101
DEFENSIVE LINE
DRILLS

Mark Snyder

ISBN: 1-57167-372-5
Library of Congress Catalog Card Number: 99-60411

Cover Design: Britt Johnson
Cover Photos: Courtesy of the University of Minnesota
Editor: David Hamburg
Production Manager: Michelle A. Summers

Coaches Choice Books is a division of: Sagamore Publishing, Inc.
                                                P.O. Box 647
                                                Champaign, IL 61824-0647
                                                Web Site: http//www.sagamorepub.com

DEDICATION

*To my best friend, my love, my
inspiration, my soul mate, my lovely
wife, Beth Snyder.*

*To my daughters, Chelsea and Lindsay,
for the great joy you bring to my life!*

ACKNOWLEDGMENTS

I am fortunate to have so many people to thank. I start with my Ironton High School coaches, Mike Burcham and Bob Lutz, who taught me how to win. I would also like to acknowledge the following people: Jon Tenuta, secondary coach at Ohio State University, who believed in me and taught me the coaching profession; Lee Moon, athletic director at the University of Wyoming, who taught me the importance of education and loyalty; Jim Tressel, head coach/athletic director at Youngstown State University, who showed me how to win championships, organize my time, and truly care about people; Glen Mason, head football coach at the University of Minnesota, for giving me the opportunity to coach in the Big Ten and for caring about my family's well-being; and Steve Axman, head football coach at Northern Arizona University, for helping me develop this manuscript.

These people helped to build my foundation at an early age, and they all have one thing in common: a dedication to fundamentals.

CONTENTS

PREFACE

In order to perform well on the playing field, a defensive lineman must be multitalented and multidimensional. He must be explosive, disciplined, and, in a way, a controlled fanatic. To get the most out of all of his defensive linemen, the coach must be creative in his choice of drills and wary of spending too much time on any one skill.

The 101 drills presented in this book have carryover into the progression of learning for effective defensive line play. These drills are position specific and are geared to the techniques a defensive lineman will have to use throughout the course of a season.

Each drill offers a terrific tool for teaching a particular attribute of defensive line play. In addition, each drill is designed to be employed by coaches at all competitive levels.

CHAPTER 1

AGILITY
DRILLS

DRILL #1: D-LINE WAVE

Objective: To help defensive linemen improve their body control and quickness.

Equipment Needed: None.

Description: Four lines of players face the coach. On the coach's command, the players in the first group should drop down on all fours, with their head up and their feet making quick, chopping movements. On the coach's directional signal, the players should execute a seat roll. After a few rolls, the coach says, "Hit it!" The players should get down on their stomachs and then get right back up and run 10 yards.

Coaching Points:

- The players should concentrate on their quickness—not on which way the coach is going to point.

- The players should compete with their teammates during this drill.

- The players should explode off the ground running.

- The coach should change up the seat rolls with lateral runs, lateral shuffles, bear crawls, and up/downs in any order.

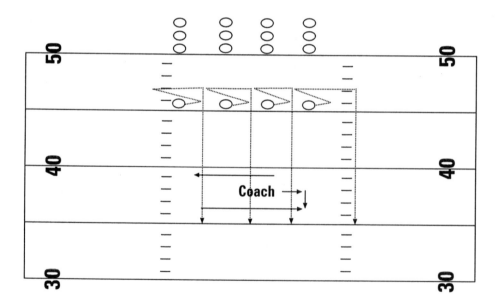

DRILL #2: D-LINE CRAB WAVE

Objective: To help defensive linemen improve their body control; to help them learn to play with their head and eyes up, even when they are fatigued; to develop their hand-foot coordination; to help them explode off the ground running.

Equipment Needed: A lined football field.

Description: Four to five lines of players position themselves five yards apart. On the coach's command, the players in the first group should get down on their stomachs and then pop up on all fours with their feet moving. The coach then alternates pointing right and left, making the players crab in different directions. After a few reps, the coach points downfield, and the players should perform a forward roll, followed by a five-yard sprint. The other groups should then run through the drill, one player at a time.

Coaching Points:

- The players should bounce up off the ground while keeping their eyes on the coach.

- The coach should emphasize quick hands and feet.

- The players should keep in mind that if they turn their rear end in the direction the coach is pointing, the rest of their body will follow.

- The players should keep their feet moving and tuck their head under for a clean forward roll.

- Rather than get up slowly, the players should explode off the ground.

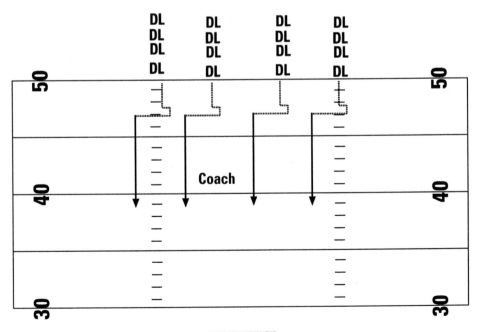

DRILL #3: HIGH KNEE

Objective: To help defensive linemen improve their body control; to help them develop rhythm; to help them increase their flexibility.

Equipment Needed: A lined football field.

Description: On the coach's command, the players in the first group should pump their knees as high and as quickly as they can, while maintaining proper arm action for 10 yards. Each group should run through the drill in the same manner.

Coaching Points:

- The players should keep their upper body erect and relaxed.

- The players should keep their knees pointed straight upfield.

- The players should strive for high knee action.

- The players should use the proper arm action, which is hip to ear.

- The players should think "pace," not "race."

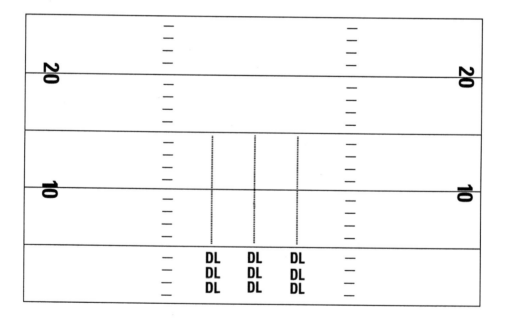

DRILL #4: QUICK STEP

Objective: To develop the ability of defensive linemen to get quick feet.

Equipment Needed: A lined football field.

Description: On the coach's command, the players in the first group up should patter their feet as quickly and as often as they can for 10 yards. The vertical movement of the players downfield should be slow, as this drill is not a race.

Coaching Points:

* The players should strive to achieve a good forward lean, with practically all their weight out in front of their body.

* Because their arms are indicators of what their legs are doing, the players should make sure their arm swings are short and quick.

* The players should keep their arms at a 90-degree angle, with their elbows in tight to their ribs and moving back and forth and breaking the plane of their body.

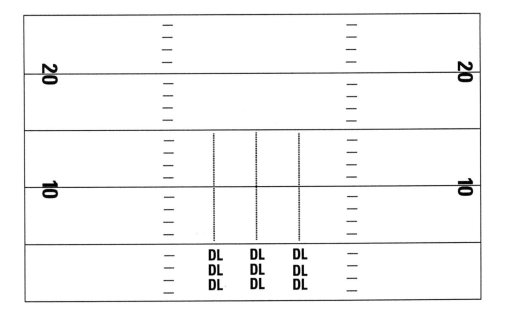

DRILL #5: HULLABALOO

Objective: To increase cardiovascular efficiency; to improve agility by using common body movements.

Equipment Needed: A lined football field.

Description: The players form a single line. The first player in line should sprint five yards, shuffle to the hash, sprint ahead another five yards, carioca to the hash, sprint ahead five more yards, backpedal to the hash, sprint ahead another five yards, bear crawl to the hash, and then burst 10 yards to the finish.

Coaching Points:

- The players should go at full speed.

- The players should work this drill in their fundamental hitting position.

- The players should change from one skill to another quickly.

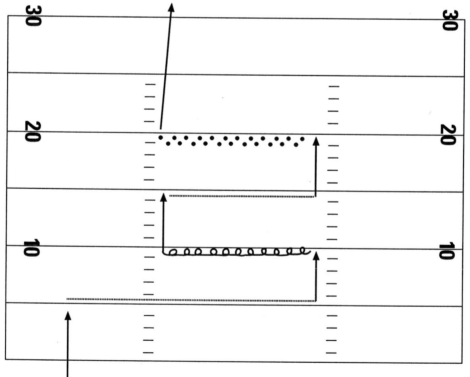

DL DL DL DL

DRILL #6: CONE

Objective: To develop the ability of defensive linemen to improve their foot quickness and their agility from a basic hitting position.

Equipment Needed: Four cones.

Description: The coach arranges the four cones in a square, 10 yards apart. This drill is run in four parts, with the first segment being a bear crawl to the first cone. Once the player gets there, he should perform a lateral shuffle to the next cone while facing the middle. He should then turn the corner and carioca to the third cone. Once he reaches the third cone, the player should burst on a sprint past the last cone.

Coaching Points:

- The players should keep in mind that, when bear crawling, they should move their hands and feet as quickly as possible.

- When converting to the shuffle, the players should be in the proper football position—not crossing over with their feet.

- When converting to the carioca, the players should maintain the proper football position and flop (i.e., twist) their hips quickly.

- The players should make sure they sprint past the last cone.

- The coach should position himself in the middle of the square so that he can more readily observe his players.

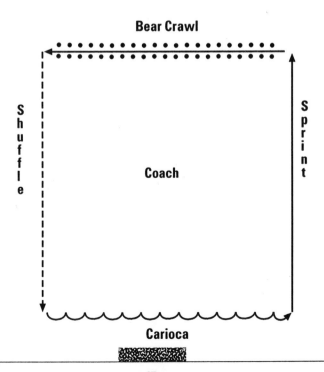

DRILL #7: LATERAL SHUFFLE

Objective: To develop the ability of defensive linemen to improve their lateral quickness from a bent-knee position.

Equipment Needed: A bucket of tennis balls.

Description: The defensive linemen begin this drill in the proper football position and on a yard line facing the coach. When the coach rolls out the first tennis ball, the first player in line should shuffle laterally to the ball, pick it up, and pitch it underhand back to the coach. As the player pitches the ball, the coach rolls another ball on a 45-degree angle five yards from the player. The player should shuffle, pick it up, and toss it back to the coach. The drill is over when fatigue sets in and the player can no longer get to the tennis ball.

Coaching Points:

- The coach should emphasize the importance of the players developing quickness from a bent-knee position.

- The coach should make sure the players take the time to pick up the ball and toss it back and work on hand-eye coordination.

- The coach should control and adjust the tempo of this drill as the players begin to tire and bobble the ball.

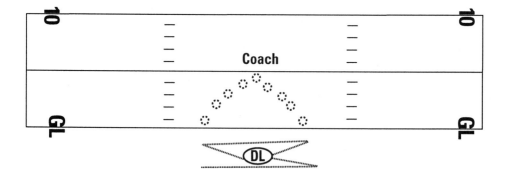

DRILL #8: CAT

Objective: To develop the ability of defensive linemen to get up off the ground after they have been cut down, and then locate their target and burst to it.

Equipment Needed: A cone; a tennis ball.

Description: Two defensive linemen lie flat on their stomachs on a yard line. On the coach's command, they should push up off the ground and race to the tennis ball.

Coaching Points:

- The coach should emphasize the importance of getting up quickly rather than slowly.

- The players should run with their weight shifted over their knees, and they should reach for their target.

- The players should compete as they race for the ball.

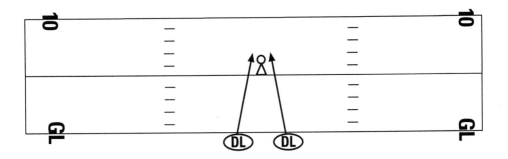

DRILL #9: 20-YARD CONE

Objective: To develop the ability of defensive linemen to increase their lateral mobility while changing directions.

Equipment Needed: Five cones; a tennis ball.

Description: The coach places two cones close together on the 10-yard line and two more cones opposite the first two cones at the goal line to form a square. In the middle of the square, at the 5-yard line, he places another cone, this one with a tennis ball on top of it. This middle cone represents the starting position for each player in the drill. Two players compete in the drill by first racing toward their cone at the 10-yard line. They should then change directions and burst 10 yards to the opposite cone at the goal line. Once again, they should reverse direction and race back to the middle cone to grab the tennis ball.

Coaching Points:

- The players should begin the drill by positioning themselves in the proper football stance.

- The players should burst with their weight over their knees so they don't have to reach down to touch the cone.

- When running from one cone to another, the players should flop their hips so that they are running in straight-line movements.

- The players should compete for the tennis ball when they get to the last cone.

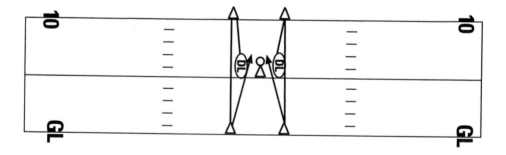

DRILL #10: SLALOM

Objective: To help defensive linemen improve their overall agility; to help them concentrate on improving their body movement from a running position; to enhance their lateral quickness.

Equipment Needed: Five agility bags; one cone.

Description: The coach places the bags two to three yards apart. He then has his players each take a turn running through the drill. Each player should zigzag around the bags, shuffling his feet and moving his hips through the bags as if he is skiing on a slalom course. After reaching the last bag, the player should burst five yards to the cone.

Coaching Points:

- The players should maintain the proper football position throughout the drill.
- The players should make sure they don't cross over with their feet; their heels should click.
- The players should use their arms to ensure proper leaning as they shuffle to the opposite direction.
- The players should take the time to clear each bag before starting in the opposite direction; their feet should never hit a bag.

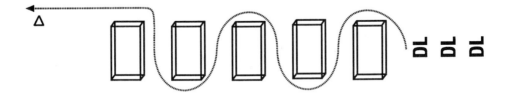

DRILL #11: EVERY FOOT

Objective: To help defensive linemen develop quick feet; to develop their ability to run over bodies from a basic hitting position.

Equipment Needed: Five agility bags; a cone.

Description: To set up this drill, the coach places five bags in a line, leaving a hole between each bag. The first player in line assumes the proper football position. On the coach's command, he runs over each bag, making sure to lead with his inside foot and to hit each hole with both feet. Once he has cleared the last bag, the player should turn and burst past the cone.

Coaching Points:

- The players should make sure they begin the drill in the proper football position and maintain that position through the bags.

- The players should make sure they do not cross over with their feet.

- If the players maintain the proper arm action, they should be able to bring their feet back up as soon as they hit the ground between bags.

- If the players fall down, the coach should discipline them to get up running and to burst past the cone.

- The coach should repeat this drill so that the players have to learn to lead with either foot.

- The coach should walk with the players through the drill to ensure that their eyes are looking up at the coach—not down at the ground.

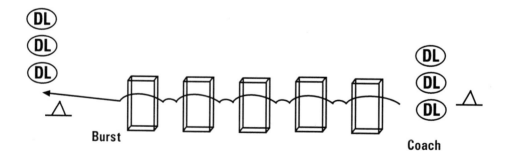

DRILL #12: ROPES: EVERY FOOT

Objective: To help the defensive linemen develop quick feet; to develop the players' ability to pick their feet up off the ground in a coordinated manner.

Equipment Needed: A set of ropes.

Description: In one single-file line, the defensive linemen run through the ropes, making sure they hit a foot down in every hole.

Coaching Points:

- The players should concentrate on picking up their feet and putting them down in the middle of each hole.

- The players should make sure their body is leaning forward and that they are using the proper arm action.

- If one player steps on the ropes, every other player's holes will start to move; therefore, each player should concentrate on precision throughout this drill.

DRILL #13: ROPES: LATERAL SHUFFLE

Objective: To help the defensive linemen develop quick feet; to develop their ability to pick their feet up off the ground while moving sideways.

Equipment Needed: A set of ropes.

Description: From a single-file line, one defensive lineman at a time runs sideways through the ropes. Each player should make sure he puts both feet down in every hole and leads with his inside foot.

Coaching Points:

- The players should concentrate on proper forward body leaning with their inside foot.

- The players should not cross over with their feet.

- The players should use proper arm action.

- The coach should remind his players that, until they have mastered this drill, it is acceptable for them to watch their feet as they run through it.

DRILL #14: JUMP ROPE

Objective: To improve the defensive linemen's hand-foot coordination; to develop their ability to maintain proper balance; to enhance their foot dexterity.

Equipment Needed: A jump rope.

Description: As they jump rope, the players should work on the following: intense concentration, precision of movement, timing, and a high degree of motor skill.

Coaching Points:

- As they turn the rope, the players should keep their upper arms close to their body.

- The players should hold their forearms down and out at a 45-degree angle, and their hands eight to 10 inches from their hips.

- The players should let their hands do most of the work in turning the rope.

- The players should circumscribe a circle of six to eight inches.

- The players should allow their feet to come off the ground just enough to let the rope slip under them.

CHAPTER 2

TACKLING DRILLS

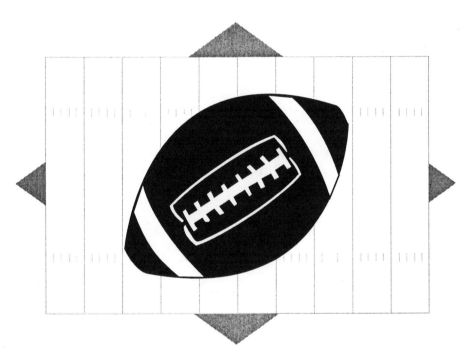

DRILL #15: PERFECT TACKLE

Objective: To develop the ability of defensive linemen to demonstrate, from a stationary position, the proper tackling techniques and fundamentals.

Equipment Needed: Three footballs; a high-jump mat (or anything soft to land on).

Description: The defender fits up (i.e., assumes the precise, proper tackling position just prior to contact with the runner) the ball carrier directly in front of the mat. On the coach's command, the defender should roll his hips and drive the ball carrier into the mat. The sides are reversed and the drill is repeated (i.e., the defender becomes the ball carrier and vice versa).

Coaching Points:

- The defender should fix his eyes on the ball carrier's chin.

- The defender's arms should be under the armpits of the ball carrier, grabbing cloth on the ball carrier's back.

- The defender should bend at his knees enough to enable him to explode into the ball carrier.

- If, on the coach's command, the defender rolls his hips properly and keeps his feet moving, he should be able to take down the ball carrier with little difficulty.

- The defender should never make a tackle with his head down.

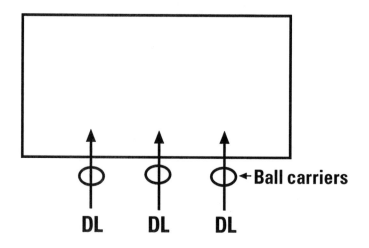

DRILL #16: FORWARD ROLL TACKLE

Objective: To develop the ability of defensive linemen to control their body, get up off the ground, locate the football, and tackle the running back.

Equipment Needed: Two cones.

Description: The defender should position himself in a three-point stance behind one of the cones. On the coach's command, he should shuffle to the next cone, perform a forward roll, and form tackle the running back. The running back should start from five yards away and then take off when the defender reaches the second cone.

Coaching Points:

- The defender should stay low, with his head up, and should not cross over with his feet.
- After executing his forward roll, the defender should explode off the ground.
- The defender should hit the ball carrier on the rise, climbing up his body and keeping his feet moving as he form tackles the ball carrier.

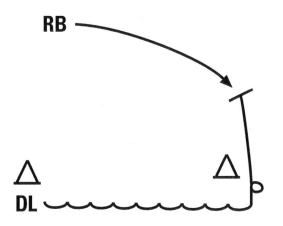

DRILL #17: EVERY FOOT/ANGLE TACKLE

Objective: To help defensive linemen learn to increase their foot speed; to develop their ability to remain disciplined enough to get up off the ground and perform a proper angle tackle.

Equipment Needed: Five agility bags; a cone.

Description: The first defensive player in line assumes the proper stance. On the coach's "hit" command, the player lead steps with his inside foot over every bag, hitting both feet down in every hole. Once he clears the last bag, the defensive player should do a seat roll, get up and locate his target (i.e., the ball carrier), and perform an angle tackle. He should keep his feet moving both on and after contact.

Coaching Points:

• The coach should make sure that each defensive player begins the drill in the proper football position and maintains that position as he steps over every bag.

• The coach should make sure the defensive players do not cross over with their feet.

• The coach should emphasize the importance of the players picking up and putting down their feet in a hurry while using the proper arm action.

• When they execute their seat roll, the players should explode off the ground rather than get up slowly.

• As they approach the ball carrier, the players should have their knees bent and should drive their helmet across the ball carrier's chest.

• The coach should make sure his defensive players use high, overexaggerated uppercuts as they grasp the ball carrier, as well as an overexaggerated chopping of their feet. (This coaching point should help the players execute the proper hip roll and enable them to climb up the ball carrier as they make the tackle.)

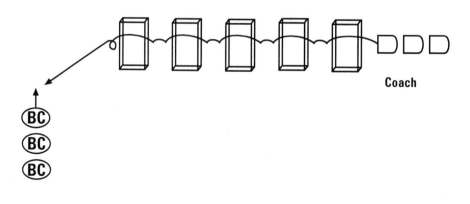

DRILL #18: CRAB ANGLE TACKLE

Objective: To help the defensive linemen improve their body control; to enhance their hand-foot coordination while on the ground; to help them develop their angle-tackling skills.

Equipment Needed: Five agility bags.

Description: In this drill, the defensive lineman must crab crawl on all fours around and between each bag. After coming out of the last bag, the player should get up off the ground running and perform an angle tackle on the ball carrier.

Coaching Points:

- The players should move their hands and feet quickly, swinging their rear end around as they change directions.

- As they come out of the last bag, the players should pop up off the ground.

- The defensive players should stay inside out on the ball carrier.

- The defensive players should get their head across the ball carrier's chest, hitting him on the rise while keeping their feet moving.

- The players should keep in mind that they should never tackle with their head down.

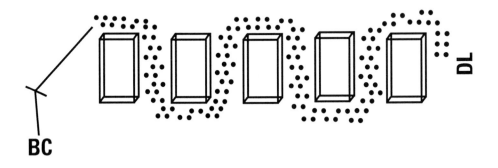

DRILL #19: FORM TACKLE

Objective: To develop the ability of defensive linemen to execute good form tackling from various angles.

Equipment Needed: Two agility bags; a football.

Description: The coach places two agility bags five yards apart. A ball carrier is positioned at the top of the bags, while a defensive lineman is positioned five yards from the ball carrier (at the bottom of the bags). On the coach's command, the ball carrier breaks either right or left or else comes straight ahead. The defender, who is keeping his feet moving, takes the proper angle and form tackles him.

Coaching Points:

- The defensive player should keep his knees bent, his head up, and his feet moving.

- If the ball carrier breaks either right or left, the defensive players should come inside out, getting his head across the ball carrier's chest and climbing up the ball carrier as he makes the tackle.

- The defensive player should grab cloth and keep his feet moving.

- If the ball carrier comes straight ahead, the defensive player should keep his head up, his knees bent, and strike the ball carrier down the cylinder of his body. The tackler should climb up the ball carrier as he tackles him and also keep his feet moving.

- The players should remember to keep their head up as they make the form tackle.

BC

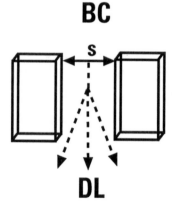

DL

DRILL #20: MIRROR TACKLING

Objective: To develop the ability of defensive linemen to learn the proper fundamentals and techniques of tackling after mirroring a running back.

Equipment Needed: Two cones; a football; a lined field.

Description: The coach places two cones 10 yards apart on a selected line of scrimmage. He then positions two tacklers at an equal distance apart between the cones and just behind the line of scrimmage. Finally, the coach positions a row of ball carriers five yards in front of the two tacklers. On the coach's command, the ball carrier jockeys back and forth in the area between the two cones. After moving back and forth a few times, the ball carrier attempts to cross the line of scrimmage as both defensive linemen tackle him and prevent him from crossing the line of scrimmage.

Coaching Points:

- The two tacklers should maintain an inside-outside relationship with the ball carrier.

- The two tacklers should keep their shoulders parallel to the line of scrimmage throughout this drill.

- The two tacklers should remember not to cross over with their feet, but instead shuffle.

- The two tacklers should try to maintain an equal distance between each other.

- The two tacklers should fit up the ball carrier and keep their feet moving.

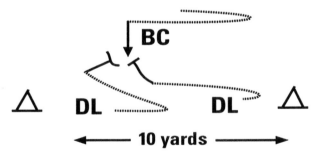

DRILL #21: BLIND MAN

Objective: To develop the ability of defensive linemen to execute proper form tackling and to maintain good peripheral vision after escaping a block.

Equipment Needed: A bell dummy; a football.

Description: Two lines of players set up opposite each other with a bell dummy placed between them. One line consists of ball carriers, while the other line consists of tacklers. Both lines are set up four yards from the bell dummy. On the coach's command, the first ball carrier in line takes two steps and then breaks either right or left. The first defender in his line should then pick up the ball carrier in his vision and execute an angle tackle.

Coaching Points:

- The defensive linemen should assume the proper football position and keep their feet moving.

- Once the opposite-color jersey shows, the tackler should accelerate to a point at which he can cut the runner off.

- The tackler should stay inside out on the ball carrier.

- The tackler should get his helmet across the ball carrier's chest, shoot his arms through and grab cloth, and climb up the ball carrier's body while keeping his feet moving.

- The tackler should remember that he cannot make the tackle with his head down.

DRILL #22: MACHINE GUN

Objective: To develop the ability of defensive linemen to successfully take on a series of blockers, find the football, and execute proper form tackling.

Equipment Needed: A football.

Description: The coach aligns three blockers three yards apart, with the ball carrier three yards behind them. The coach has the defender face the offensive players from three yards away. On the coach's command, the defender attempts to engage and disengage each blocker. After disengaging the last blocker, the defender should form tackle the ball carrier.

Coaching Points:

- The defender should maintain proper balance and body control.

- The defender should keep his feet "live" and moving and should keep his knees bent.

- The coach should have his defenders work on different types of "fits" (e.g., frontal, shoulder, forearm lift).

- When tackling the ball carrier, the defender should hit him down the cylinder of his body. At the same time, the defender should keep his head up, climb up the ball carrier, and overexaggerate his foot movement.

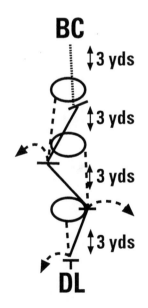

DRILL #23: GOAL-LINE TACKLE

Objective: To develop the ability of defensive linemen to tackle successfully at the goal line.

Equipment Needed: Four cones; a goal line.

Description: The coach aligns a running back and a defensive lineman three yards apart, inside a square made from the four cones. The drill consists of the defender standing on the goal line and attempting to keep the running back from scoring.

Coaching Points:

- The tackler should maintain a solid base and keep his feet moving.
- The tackler should meet the running back as deep as possible from the goal line.
- The tackler should take on the running back high and engage as much surface on him as possible while keeping his feet moving.
- As with all drills and live tackling, the defender must always remember to keep his head up when making the tackle.

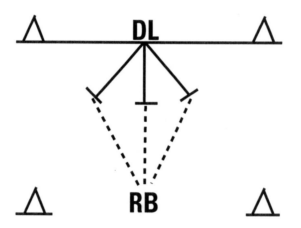

CHAPTER 3

RUN-PLAY DRILLS

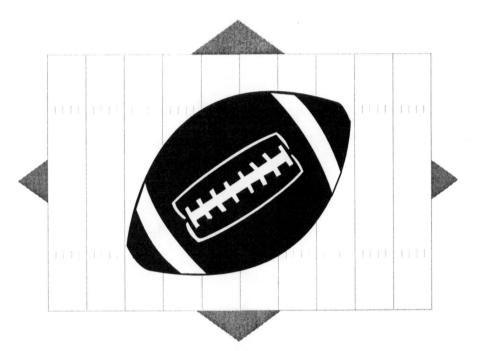

DRILL #24: EXPLOSION ESCAPE

Objective: To develop the ability of defensive linemen to play with their heads up; to enhance their ability to hit on the rise; to develop their ability to roll their hips, to use proper hand placement, and to escape their blocker while squaring their shoulders back up.

Equipment Needed: A two-man sled.

Description: The coach positions two defensive linemen in the proper three-point stance, facing the sled. On the coach's "hit" command, both defenders hit the sled simultaneously. The front of the sled should come up off the ground while they pump their feet and drive it backwards. The coach then gives an "escape" command, at which point the two linemen should perform an escape technique to a predetermined side.

Coaching Points:

- The linemen should both deliver an explosive stab to the pits of the dummy, hitting it on the rise.

- The linemen should roll their hips and press the dummy for separation.

- The linemen should drive their feet explosively and quickly as they hit and drive the sled.

- When the "escape" command is given, the linemen should employ a rip or throw technique while escaping from the sled

- The coach should emphasize to the linemen that they square their shoulders back up to the line of scrimmage in order to make a play.

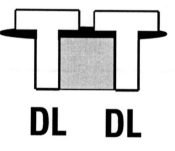

DL   DL

DRILL #25: FIVE-MAN SLED

Objective: To develop the ability of defensive linemen to explode into the ball carrier while rolling their hips; to enhance their hand quickness, including the proper techniques of hand placement and the stab.

Equipment Needed: A five-man sled.

Description: The coach has the defender line up two yards outside the first pad in the proper football position. On the coach's "hit" command, the defensive lineman begins a lateral shuffle to the first pad and executes a blow delivery technique to the pad. On the recoil, he shuffles laterally to the next pad, until he has executed the technique on all five pads.

Coaching Points:

- As he goes down the pads, the defender should take a six-inch jab step with his right root (i.e., he takes a power step).

- The defender should hit each pad on the rise and roll his hips.

- Instead of winding up before stabbing, the defender should shoot his hands explosively and quickly on the stab.

- The defender should keep his shoulders square throughout the drill.

- If he desires, the defender can incorporate a rip move as an option on the last pad.

- The defender, when coming back down the sled, should use his left foot on the power step.

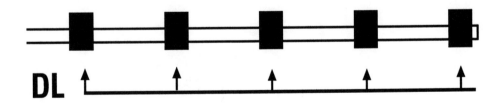

DRILL #26: SLED PUNCH

Objective: To develop the upper-body mechanics of defensive linemen, including their hip roll, their hand placement, and their separation.

Equipment Needed: A one-man sled/pad.

Description: The first defensive lineman begins the drill positioned slightly less than an arm's length from the pad. He has his knees on the ground, with his toes coiled behind. His arms are relaxed, and his hands are at the height of the jersey number. On the coach's command, the defensive lineman thrusts his hips forward while striking outward, and slightly upward, with his initial punch to the pad.

Coaching Points:

- The player should concentrate on quickness in his hands and his hips.
- The player should keep his shoulders pressed back and his chin up.
- The player's thumbs should be up at 1 o'clock and 11 o'clock.

DRILL #27: THREE-POINT EXPLOSION

Objective: To develop the ability of defensive linemen to get their lower body to work in concert with their upper body when delivering a blow.

Equipment Needed: A one-man sled/pad.

Description: A defensive lineman begins the drill positioned in the proper three-point stance, head-up on the sled. On the coach's command, the player takes a six-inch power step, engaging the sled simultaneously with his hands and rolling his hips.

Coaching Points:

- The player should try to be quick with his step, his hands, and his hips.

- The player should keep his shoulders pressed back and his chin up.

- The player should position his thumbs at 1 o'clock and 11 o'clock.

- The player should be explosive with his stab.

DRILL #28: SHADE EXPLOSION

Objective: To develop the ability of defensive linemen to get their lower body to work in concert with their upper body when delivering a blow from a shade on the offensive line—disengaging the block into the proper gap.

Equipment Needed: A one-man sled/pad.

Description: The defensive lineman should be shaded either right or left on the sled. On the coach's command, the player takes a six-inch power step to the middle of the sled, engaging the sled simultaneously with his hands and rolling his hips. After separation is completed, the player should escape the sled with a rip move.

Coaching Points:

- The player should strive for quickness in his step, his hands, and his hips.

- The player should stab his inside hand to the middle of the pad, with his off, or outside, hand on the edge of the pad for gap control.

- When he is shaded, the defensive lineman should always step with his inside foot.

- The player should strive to be quick and explosive when ripping the sled.

DRILL #29: TWO-POINT EXPLOSION

Objective: To develop the ability of defensive linemen to properly deliver a blow and to explode as a result of rolling the hips; to enhance their ability to use the proper power foot, as well as the proper hand placement.

Equipment Needed: Five agility bags.

Description: On the "hit" command, the defensive lineman should lead with his onside foot into each hole. Once he is in the hole, the blocker should come at him, standing tall and showing his numbers at 80 percent. The defender should then execute a frontal technique, exploding up through the blocker and continuing this maneuver through each hole.

Coaching Points:

- The defensive lineman should keep his weight over his knees, with his tail down throughout the whole drill, or else he will be unable to find any power-producing angles.

- The defensive lineman should let the blocker come to him, and he should also guard against overextension.

- The defensive lineman should explode up through the blocker, bringing his power foot and rolling his hips as he stabs the blocker in the chest.

- The coach should make sure that the defensive lineman forms a triangle with his head and both his hands as he makes contact. (This contact is known as a frontal.)

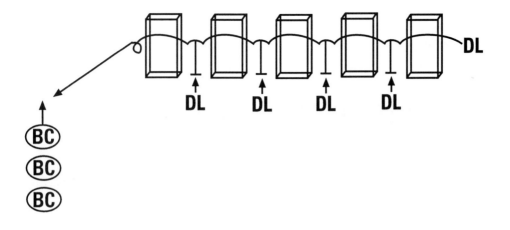

DRILL #30: VITAL TECHNIQUE

Objective: To develop the ability of defensive linemen to understand the importance of using proper technique when having to defeat a block and make a tackle on either side of them; to develop in them the ability to concentrate on defeating a block before finding the ball carrier.

Equipment Needed: Four cones; two footballs.

Description: The coach positions a defensive lineman over an offensive lineman in head-up technique. He also positions two ball carriers eight yards deep and opposite each other, as well as two sets of cones five yards from the defender. On the snap of the ball, the defender should defeat the block and make the tackle on the ball carrier to whom the coach points.

Coaching Points:

- The defender should move on the movement of the offensive lineman.
- The coach should check whether the defender is using the proper blow delivery, separation, and disengagement.
- The defender should take the proper pursuit angle inside out after disengagement.
- The defender should hit the ball carrier while on the rise, and he should overexaggerate the movement of his feet.

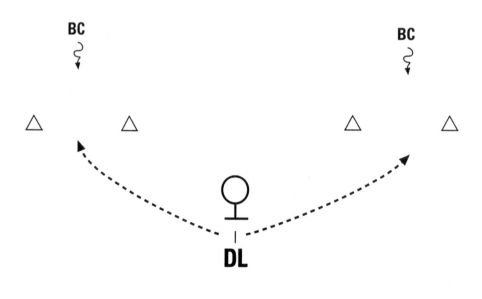

DRILL #31: BASE

Objective: To enhance the ability of defensive linemen to work from a strong base and to use the proper fit.

Equipment Needed: A six-foot-long two-by-four.

Description: The coach places an offensive lineman and a defensive lineman two yards apart and straddling the two-by-four. The drill begins on the movement of the offensive lineman. Upon contact with one another, if one player doesn't have a strong base, he will step on the board and the drill will thus be over. If both players employ a good base and a proper fit, their confrontation will result in a stalemate, and a quick whistle will be blown.

Coaching Points:

- The defensive lineman should move on the movement of the offensive lineman.

- The defender should hit on the rise while using the proper fit.

- The defender should lock out the offensive lineman and remember to churn his feet while using a strong base.

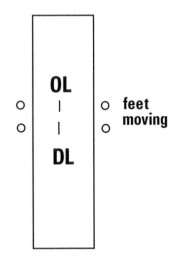

DRILL #32: CHUTE

Objective: To develop the ability of defensive linemen to defeat the blocker over them before reacting to the ball carrier.

Equipment Needed: A painted chute field; a football.

Description: Two vertical lines are painted five yards apart and six yards long, with the alley opening up after six yards. The running back must stay between those lines after receiving the ball from the quarterback. On the quarterback's signal, the defensive lineman must get off the block and make the tackle. The running back has a two-way go on either side of the blocker.

Coaching Points:

- The defender should get off on the ball and deliver a blow, then separate and disengage the offensive lineman.

- The defender should make sure he defeats the offensive lineman first, and he can help himself by using a strong base.

- If the defender starts reaching before getting off the block, the offensive lineman will have a pancake block.

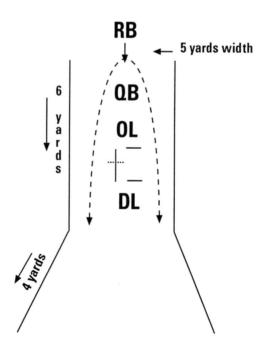

DRILL #33: TRIANGLE

Objective: To develop the ability of defensive linemen to explode into a blocker, regardless of the angle from which the blocker is coming, by properly using a shoulder forearm lift and a frontal technique with his hands.

Equipment Needed: None.

Description: The defensive lineman assumes a two-point stance facing the three men who represent the offensive blockers. The two outside blockers are positioned three yards away from the defender, while the blocker in the middle is positioned four yards away. The coach will begin the drill by pointing to one of the three blockers and having the defensive lineman attack that blocker. The defender should use the proper technique on that blocker and then return to his original position, keeping his feet moving as he prepares to take on the next blocker. After five or six repetitions, the coach should have the next player perform the drill, with each player moving to his right.

Coaching Points:

- To enhance his explosion, the defender should keep his weight over his knees and his tail down.

- The defender should attack the blocker—not vice versa.

- When attacking either outside blocker, the defender should use a shoulder forearm lift and step into the blocker, rolling his hips and hitting the blocker while on the rise.

- When attacking the middle blocker, the defender should use a frontal technique, exploding up through the blocker, bringing his power foot, and rolling his hips as he stabs him in the chest.

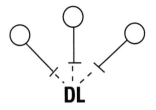

DRILL #34: CROSS-FACE

Objective: To develop the ability of defensive linemen to properly and successfully engage an angle block and cross-face the blocker to the ball carrier.

Equipment Needed: A cone; a football.

Description: The coach positions a defensive lineman in a two-point stance between two blockers who are tilted in at a 45-degree angle, five yards apart. The coach places a cone three yards in front of the defender and a ball carrier two yards behind the cone. On the coach's command, the ball carrier approaches the cone and breaks either right or left. When the ball carrier reaches the cone, the appropriate blocker should attack the defensive lineman. The defensive lineman, meanwhile, should react to the ball carrier and cross-face the blocker and fit up the ball carrier.

Coaching Points:

- Once the running back chooses his direction, the defender should pick up the down blocker in his vision.

- The defender should turn and butt up the blocker on his outside half, pressing his outside hand into the blocker's chest and turning his own shoulders back to parallel to the line of scrimmage.

- The defender should get his shoulders squared back up to the line of scrimmage as quickly as possible and escape the block with a violent throw or rip.

- The defender should fit up the ball carrier, hitting him while on the rise and keeping his feet moving.

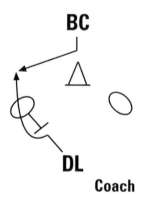

DRILL #35: DUCKWALK

Objective: To develop the ability of defensive linemen to move and play low with a strong, low base.

Equipment Needed: A set of chutes.

Description: The coach sets up his players in two lines and duckwalks them straight through the chutes.

Coaching Points:

- The coach should consider using this drill as a good warm-up drill.
- The players should overexaggerate the bend in their knees so that their butt is almost touching the ground.
- The players should always keep their head and their eyes up.

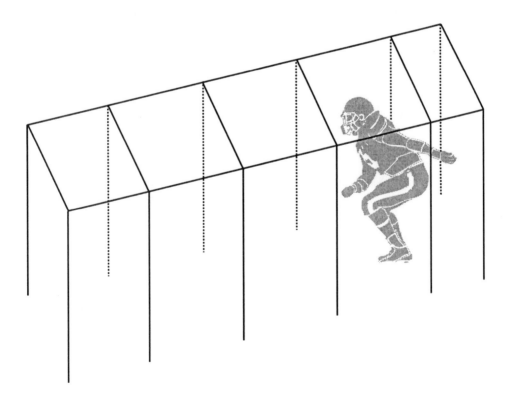

DRILL #36: DUCKWALK (SIDEWAYS)

Objective: To develop the ability of defensive linemen to move laterally with a strong, low base.

Equipment Needed: A set of chutes.

Description: The coach sets up his players in two lines facing sideways in the chutes. He then duckwalks them sideways through the chutes.

Coaching Points:

- The coach should consider using this drill as a good warm-up drill.

- The players should overexaggerate the bend in their knees so that their butt is almost touching the ground.

- The players should always keep their head and their eyes up.

- To add some fun to the drill, the coach should have the linemen quack as they go through the chutes.

DRILL #37: LEVERAGE/FIT/ESCAPE

Objective: To develop the ability of defensive linemen to properly strike an offensive lineman as he comes out of his stance; to enhance their ability to strike with a good fit while on the rise; to help them strengthen their base.

Equipment Needed: A chute; a six-foot-long two-by-four; a football.

Description: The coach positions a defensive lineman in the chute with an offensive lineman who is near the edge of the board. On the movement of the ball, the defensive lineman should come out of his stance with a strong base, clearing the front bar of the chute. He should then drive the offensive lineman down the board and escape the block as he clears the board.

Coaching Points:

- The defensive lineman should come out low and with his eyes up. After clearing the bar and fitting up the offensive lineman, he should overexaggerate the movement of his feet.

- The defensive lineman should maintain a strong base and should never step on the board.

- The offensive lineman should be going at about half speed. The defensive lineman should be going at full speed as he walks the offensive lineman down the board.

- The defensive lineman should make a clean escape at the end of the drill.

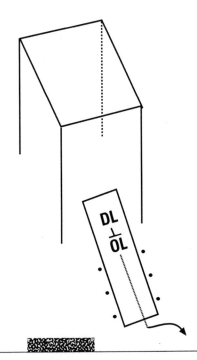

DRILL #38: PUSH/PULL

Objective: To develop the ability of defensive linemen to fight pressure with pressure and invert the offensive lineman's shoulder pads to the line of scrimmage, thus taking away his power angles on both scoop and reach blocks.

Equipment Needed: None.

Description: The coach fits up each defensive lineman with an offensive lineman in a two-point stance. The offensive linemen are standing erect, with the coach standing behind the defenders to give instruction. The defensive linemen are to close their eyes as the coach points to either the right or the left. The offensive linemen have their hands on the defenders' shoulder pads. When the coach points, they should push on the shoulder pads. When the defensive linemen feel the push, they should push back and pull with the opposite arm, turning the shoulders of the offensive linemen.

Coaching Points:

- The defensive linemen should have a lot of bend in their knees, as well as proper hand placement on the breast of the offensive linemen.

- When their shoulder is pushed, the defenders should push back and keep their feet moving in the direction of that push.

- The defensive linemen should pull with their other hand. This action will move the offensive linemen's other shoulder into them and cause the offensive linemen's shoulders to turn.

- By having the defensive linemen close their eyes, the coach is taking away the element of guessing and, in the process, forcing the players to rely on the feeling of pressure.

DRILL #39: PRESS

Objective: To teach defensive linemen the progression of separation by having them press the blocker five times.

Equipment Needed: None.

Description: The coach positions the defensive lineman in his technique over an offensive lineman. The coach begins the drill by having the offensive lineman zone block the defender high. The defensive lineman then locks up with him and presses him five times before escaping and chopping his feet.

Coaching Points:

- The defender must strive for separation so that the offensive blocker will have trouble holding him.

- The defender should stab the offensive blocker in the breastplate of the shoulder pads and grab hold.

- The defender should keep his thumbs up at 1 o'clock and 11 o'clock.

- Once he has a firm grip on the blocker, the defender should begin to press and bring the blocker back to him five times.

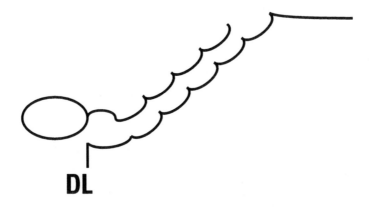

DL

DRILL #40: RECOIL

Objective: To develop the ability of defensive linemen to use the proper fundamentals and techniques for shedding a blocker, pursuing a ball carrier, and executing a tackle.

Equipment Needed: A football; a lined field.

Description: The coach sets up two rows of linemen in front-facing positions adjacent to the sideline and across a selected line of scrimmage. The coach designates the players in one row as blockers and those in the other row as defenders. One yard separates the blockers and the defenders. A ball carrier is positioned five yards deep. On the coach's command, the first two drill participants (i.e., one offensive lineman and one defender) should break down in the proper football position. This drill begins with a frontal technique by the defender as the blocker comes at him. After executing the frontal, the defender recoils to a basic hitting position one yard from the blocker and attacks with a frontal again. After five recoils, the defender should perform an angle tackle on the running back.

Coaching Points:

- The defender should maintain the proper football position throughout.

- The defender should buzz his feet after each recoil (i.e., he should move his feet quickly in place).

- The defender should strike on the rise after each recoil and engagement with the blocker.

- The defender should keep his shoulders square to the line of scrimmage.

- The defender should tackle the ball carrier on the rise, shooting his arms through and keeping his feet moving (i.e., running his feet).

- This is not a race—the coach should emphasize fundamentals and techniques.

- The defender should never make a tackle with his head down.

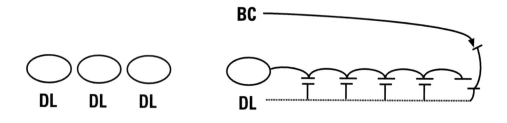

DRILL #41: ANTI-SCOOP

Objective: To develop the ability of defensive linemen to use the proper technique when playing a scoop block.

Equipment Needed: None.

Description: The coach sets up the drill so that a defensive lineman is shaded on an offensive lineman in the proper technique. He then positions another offensive lineman outside the first offensive lineman, and the second offensive lineman performs a scoop block with a one-to-two-foot split.

Coaching Points:

- The defender should attack the immediate threat first—the offensive lineman on whom he is shaded.

- The defender should move on movement, fit his eyes on the clavicle of the offensive lineman, and also shoot his inside hand to the blocker's breastplate.

- The defender should run the blocker down the line of scrimmage, flattening him out so he cannot climb to the linebacker.

- If the offensive lineman escapes the defender and climbs to the linebacker, the defender must play the second scooper with his off hand on any surface he can get to.

- The defender should now flatten down the line of scrimmage and replace the linebacker.

- It is this author's opinion that the scoop block is the hardest blocking combo for a defensive lineman to handle; therefore, it must be practiced every day.

DT

DRILL #42: ANTI-REACH

Objective: To develop the ability of defensive linemen to use the proper technique when playing a reach block.

Equipment Needed: None.

Description: The coach sets up the drill so that a defensive lineman is shaded on an offensive lineman in the proper technique. He then positions another offensive lineman inside the first offensive lineman, and he performs a reach block with a one-to-two-foot split.

Coaching Points:

- The defender should attack the offensive lineman who is aligned across from him. He should focus his eyes on the clavicle of the offensive player and shoot his inside arm to the blocker's breastplate.

- Once the defender recognizes the reach block by the inside blocker, he should start to press his off (outside) hand, which is against the blocker's shoulder pad.

- The defender should pull his inside hand, which is against the blocker's breastplate. This move will provide a push/pull and force the offensive lineman's shoulders to turn, thus taking away his power.

- If the defender encounters an overreach, he should come under the offensive lineman and get vertical right away so the inside reaching lineman cannot get a piece of him.

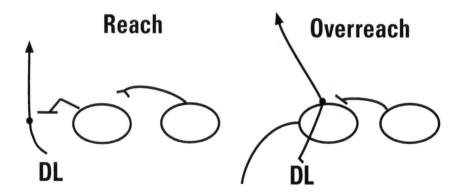

DRILL #43: ANTI-DOUBLE-TEAM

Objective: To develop the ability of defensive linemen to play a double-team.

Equipment Needed: None.

Description: The coach sets up the drill with a defensive lineman shaded on the offensive lineman in the proper technique. He then positions another offensive lineman outside the first offensive lineman to establish the double-team with a one-to-two-foot split.

Coaching Points:

- The coach should emphasize to his defensive linemen that, most of the time, pre-snap tight splits by the offensive linemen will give away the double-team block.

- The defender should attack the most immediate threat first—the offensive lineman he is shade on—and attempt to defeat him.

- Once he feels pressure from the side or the back, the defender should brace himself and get his feet moving.

- If the double-team begins to move him, the defender should drop his inside knee and turn his upper body so as to make himself small in an attempt to split the double-team.

- If one of the double-teamers comes off the block, the defender should let the force of the other block push him into that gap. In short, the defender should always think about keeping himself as a factor on the play.

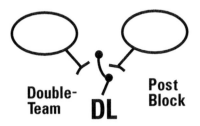

Double-Team **DL** **Post Block**

DRILL #44: DEFENSIVE TACKLE ANTI-TRAP

Objective: To develop the ability of defensive tackles to use the proper technique and to react properly to a quick trap.

Equipment Needed: None.

Description: A center and two offensive guards are needed in this drill, with the defensive tackle being an outside shade on one of the guards. The coach stands behind the defensive tackle and begins the drill by instructing the three offensive linemen to perform a blocking scheme. The two types of quick traps are the "influence" trap and the "veer" trap.

Coaching Points:

- The defensive lineman should attack the clavicle of the immediate threat (i.e., the offensive guard) first.

- As the guard blocks down, the defensive lineman should squeeze down with him, looking for the next threat. This particular blocking scheme is the veer trap.

- Once the next threat is encountered (i.e., the pulling guard), the defensive lineman should attack the inside half of the guard, eliminating the trap and making the ball bounce outside.

- If the guard (i.e., the first threat) quick sets and releases outside, the defensive lineman should look back inside and go meet the opposite pulling guard and "trap the trapper" (collision him) and create a pile. This blocking scheme is the influence trap.

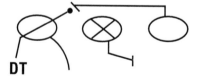
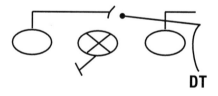

DRILL #45: MULTI-READ

Objective: To develop the ability of defensive linemen to understand reaction time and use the proper technique versus multiple series of combination blocks.

Equipment Needed: None.

Description: The coach aligns a defensive lineman so that he is shaded on the offensive lineman in the proper technique. He then positions another offensive lineman outside the first offensive lineman to facilitate combination blocks. The coach stands behind the defensive lineman and instructs the offensive lineman to either double-team, reach, scoop, or pass set the defensive lineman.

Coaching Points:

- The defender should key the first threat—the offensive lineman who is shade on—for initial movement.

- The defender's mind-set has to be one of defeating the first threat first.

- After he defeats the first block, the defender's reaction time is essential.

- The responses taught in this drill are learned responses; therefore, in order to ensure that they are learned properly, the coach should have his players work on them every day.

- This drill is useful for both defensive tackles and defensive ends.

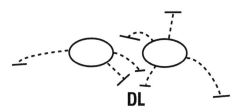

DRILL #46: DEFENSIVE END ANTI-KICK-OUT

Objective: To develop the ability of defensive ends to use the proper technique for spilling (i.e., coming under) a kick-out block by the fullback; to improve their awareness so that they are able to find secondary threats and also cancel gaps.

Equipment Needed: A strip (hose).

Description: The coach aligns the defensive end at the end of the strip over a tackle or a tight end to set up the initial key recognition. Next, the coach aligns the fullback three yards behind the imaginary center. On the coach's command, either the tackle or the tight end steps down, and the fullback comes inside out in an attempt to kick out the defensive end.

Coaching Points:

- The initial key is either the tackle or the tight end, so the defender should let one of those two players take him to the fullback.

- Once the offensive lineman is no longer a threat to block him, the defender should find the fullback and meet him as deep as possible.

- The defender should take the inside half of the fullback's body with a shoulder forearm lift.

- As contact is made, the defender should roll his hips to gain maximum power.

- If the defensive end exhibits quick reaction time, all he needs in order to be successful is a stalemate.

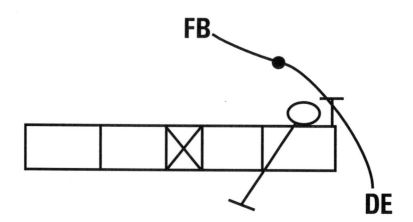

DRILL #47: DEFENSIVE END ANTI–LONG TRAP

Objective: To develop the ability of defensive ends to recognize traps off of an initial pass key by an offensive lineman.

Equipment Needed: None.

Description: Two offensive tackles align seven yards apart, with the defensive end set up in a pass-rush stance over one of them. The offensive tackle who is covered up will pass set for two counts and then release inside. The off tackle should then pull and attempt to kick out the defensive end.

Coaching Points:

- The defender should get off of the football and simulate a game-like vertical push up the field.

- As the pass-rush technique is about to be used and the offensive tackle releases inside, the defender should plant his outside foot for maximum drive.

- The defender should turn his hips and knees down the line of scrimmage. He should work back into the line.

- The defender should try to get to the inside half of the offensive tackle so he can eliminate the trap and make the ball bounce outside.

- The long trap is an offense's best weapon against a good pass rusher, because it slows him down.

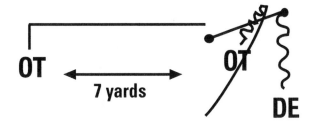

DRILL #48: INSIDE ZONE/BOOTLEG

Objective: To develop the ability of defensive ends to react quickly to bootlegs off of inside zone fakes.

Equipment Needed: A strip (hose); a football.

Description: The coach aligns the open-side defensive end over an offensive tackle for his initial key. The coach stands behind the defensive end and instructs the backfield players to fake an inside zone play. The offensive tackle blocks down every time, and the fullback either kicks out the defensive end for inside zone, or he bypasses him and runs a flat route for bootlegs. The defensive end then has to distinguish whether the play is an inside zone or a bootleg. The offense should change up between run and pass to keep the defensive end honest.

Coaching Points:

- The defender should squeeze down the line of scrimmage on the initial down block by the tackle.

- The defender should pick up the second threat—the fullback.

- The defender should work to the inside half of the fullback to bounce the inside zone and cancel his gap.

- If the fullback bypasses the defensive end, the play is a bootleg.

- The defender should work flat down the line of scrimmage until he gains horizontal leverage on the quarterback, and he should then climb vertically for the sack.

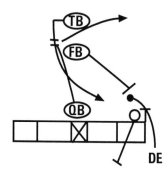 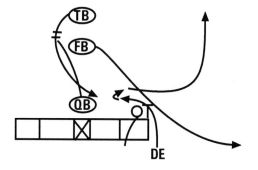

DRILL #49: PROGRESSION READS

Objective: To teach the defensive end the importance of reading initial keys, playing tough on the tight end, recognizing series of actions, and progressing from one threat to another while consistently using proper technique.

Equipment Needed: A strip (hose); a football.

Description: The coach starts the progression by having the defensive end play just the tight end, facing a combination of reach, drive, cutoff, and pass blocks. The coach then progresses to the possibility of from one to four blockers who could block the defensive end on a given play. The coach stands behind the defender and instructs the offensive players as to what he wants them to do—according to what strategy the opponent for that week tends to use to attack the defensive end. The coach then tells the defender what front he wants him to employ. Next, the defensive end reads his keys and performs the techniques required for that play.

Coaching Points:

- The defensive end should start the drill in the proper stance and use a strong base to enhance his explosiveness.

- The defensive end should mirror step with the tight end, shooting his hands and playing him tough until the tight end is no longer a threat.

- The defensive end should not get reached or driven off the ball; he should squeeze all down blocks.

- Once the tight end is no longer a threat to him, the defensive end should react to what he sees. If his next threat is a back or a pulling lineman, the defensive end should attack him tight down the line of scrimmage, attacking him using the required technique. The defensive end's technique will be determined by his gap responsibility.

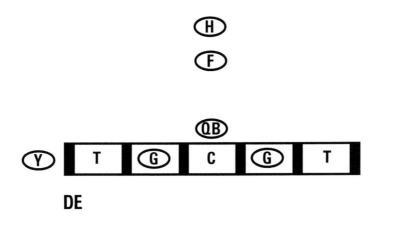

DRILL #50: CUT

Objective: To develop the ability of defensive ends to play cut blocks using their hands; to develop the ability to keep their eyes on the blocker until he has been defeated; to underscore the importance of keeping blockers off their legs.

Equipment Needed: A lined field.

Description: The coach has three blockers align three yards apart horizontally and two yards apart vertically. The first blocker should be in a four-point stance, the second blocker should be in a three-point stance, and the third blocker should be in a two-point stance. The defender begins the drill by beginning a shuffle, and each blocker fires out at his outside leg in an attempt to cut him after he comes off the previous block.

Coaching Points:

- The defensive end should use his hands to make contact with the blocker.

- The defensive end should remember to keep his knees bent; he should never have straight legs.

- The blocker should be kept on the inside leg of the defensive end.

- The eyes of the defensive end should stay on the blocker until the blocker is defeated.

- If the blocker does get to the inside leg of the defensive end, a drop step should be performed to get around him. The end should keep in mind that in order to gain ground, he must give ground.

DRILL #51: OPTION

Objective: To develop the ability of defensive ends to slow-play the option, to see the ball pitched, and to turn and run the line horizontally, meeting the running back at the line of scrimmage.

Equipment Needed: A hose or strip; three cones; a lined field; a football.

Description: On the snap, the quarterback options the defensive end. If the ball is pitched and the running back gets to the 10-yard cone before being touched, the offense gets one point. If the defensive end touches him, the defense gets one point. If the quarterback gets to the 10-yard cone without being touched, it is worth two points to the offense. If the defensive end touches the quarterback before he pitches the ball, the defense is awarded two points. If a fumble occurs in any phase, the defense receives six points. If the defense recovers the fumble, it receives 12 points.

Coaching Points:

- The defensive end should change up the way he plays the quarterback; he should try not to give the quarterback the same look every time.

- The defensive end should focus on making the offense execute the pitch phase and not letting the quarterback score.

- The defensive end should turn and run the line when the ball is pitched; he should cut the running back off at the pass.

- To help cause an errant pitch from the quarterback, the defensive end should swipe the quarterback's outside arm.

- When slow-playing the quarterback, the defensive end should get his inside arm up in the quarterback's face and stay on his own side of the line of scrimmage as he shuffles with the quarterback.

- This drill is an exciting teaching tool, especially if the head coach keeps score.

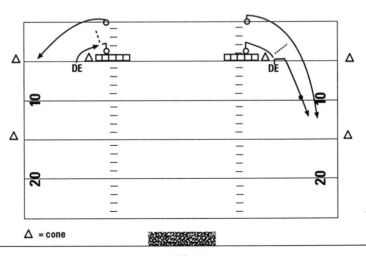

△ = cone

DRILL #52: DEFENSIVE LINEMAN PURSUIT

Objective: To develop the ability of defensive linemen to take proper pursuit angles on all outside run plays.

Equipment Needed: Four cones; one lined field; one football.

Description: The coach positions the defensive linemen in their normal alignment. On the snap of the ball, the linemen do a grass drill (i.e., hit down on the ground with their stomachs) and then get up and run around the appropriate cone and to the coach. The following assignments tell the defensive linemen which cone to go to with play at them and play away from them: The noseguard always runs around cone three, whether it's play to him or play away from him. The defensive tackles run around cone two with play at them, but cone three on play away from them. The defensive ends run around cone one with play to them, and cone four with play away from them. When the defensive linemen are finished rounding the cone, they should burst to the coach for a breakdown.

Coaching Points:

- The linemen should get up off of the ground quickly.

- The linemen should turn their knees and hips and burst around the cone.

- When the linemen arrive at the coach, their feet should be moving in a good football position until the coach breaks them down.

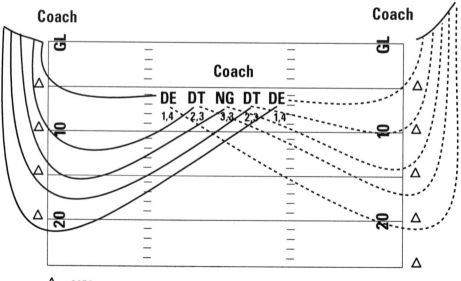

△ = cone

DRILL #53: TAKEOFF/PURSUIT

Objective: To develop the ability of defensive linemen to get off on ball movement while using a strong base, successfully penetrating the backfield, and chasing the ball carrier at the proper angle.

Equipment Needed: A football; a lined field.

Description: Four or five defensive linemen crowd a football four yards from a yard line. The coach simulates the play of a quarterback and barks out signals. When the ball is snapped, the defensive linemen should burst out of their stance to the yard line. Once the defensive linemen get to the line, the second coach gives them a directional point, either right or left.

Coaching Points:

- The defensive linemen should ground the ball as much as possible without being offside.

- The coach should look for a toe to instep stagger about shoulder-width apart.

- The defensive linemen should have their inside hand down and their inside foot back.

- The coach should watch the first two steps and make sure the players do not overstride.

- The coach should emphasize getting both feet back on the ground after takeoff with a good base.

- The coach should make sure the rush men finish on the yard line in order to ensure a proper pursuit angle to the ball.

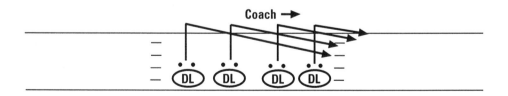

DRILL #54: NOSEGUARD EXPLOSION

Objective: To develop the ability of the noseguard to use the proper fundamentals and techniques in defeating the center's reach blocks and stepping over bodies as he goes down the line of scrimmage.

Equipment Needed: Four agility bags; a football.

Description: The coach aligns a quarterback and an offensive center in the middle of four agility bags, two to the right and two to the left. The middle hole should be four yards wide. The coach positions the noseguard over the offensive center and, on the snap of the ball, the center reaches either right or left. Once the noseguard gets a directional read (i.e., reach block, right or left), he should play off the reach and step over two bags and redirect up the field.

Coaching Points:

- The noseguard should position himself in the proper stance.

- The noseguard should strive for a quick reaction time to the offensive center's reach block and should also be quick when he separates himself from the center.

- The noseguard should concentrate on picking his feet up when stepping over the agility bags so he doesn't trip on them.

- The noseguard should get off of the center's block cleanly and keep his shoulders square throughout the drill.

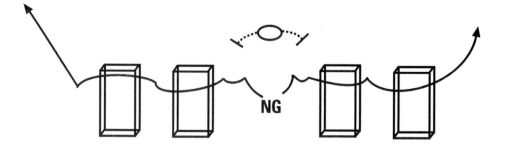

DRILL #55: DEFENSIVE END REVERSE

Objective: To develop the ability of defensive ends to properly and successfully eliminate all reverses.

Equipment Needed: A lined football field; a football.

Description: The coach sets up an offensive backfield with a wide receiver to the opposite side of the defensive end. The coach also aligns the defensive end over an offensive tackle. On the coach's command, the offense simulates a play away, with the wide receiver coming around for the reverse. The offensive tackle veer releases inside and loops around the defensive end for the cleanup block.

Coaching Points:

- The defensive end should shuffle down the line of scrimmage to help himself with the reverse after the down block by the offensive tackle.

- Once the reversing wide receiver is picked up in the visual triangle, the defensive end should work vertically up the field.

- The defensive end should turn his shoulders away from the line of scrimmage; this move will serve to turn his back to all cleanup blockers.

- The defensive end should make the reversing wide receiver turn back into the line of scrimmage; this move will allow the rest of the defense to recover and have a shorter distance to travel for the tackle.

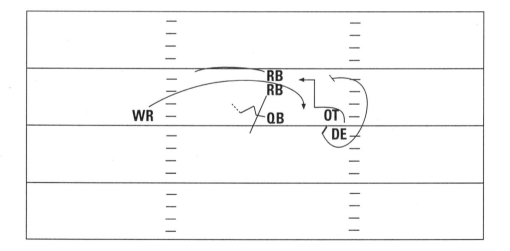

DRILL #56: GOAL-LINE GAP CHARGE

Objective: To develop the ability of defensive linemen to use the proper technique on goal-line gap charges.

Equipment Needed: A football.

Description: The coach aligns two offensive linemen shoe to shoe (two inches apart) in a three-point stance. He also positions a defensive lineman in the middle of the two shoes in a four-point stance. On ball movement, the defender should blow the gap as the offensive linemen try to double-team him into the end zone.

Coaching Points:

- The defensive lineman should keep his back flat and his nose six inches off the ground.

- The coach should remind his players of the importance of getting off on ball movement quickly in order to ensure successful front play.

- The defender should keep his aiming point at one yard deep across the line of scrimmage.

- The defensive lineman should explode out of his stance and try to get his head gear between the legs of the offensive linemen as they land on their belly.

- This drill will teach defensive linemen to cut the offensive linemen and also allow the linebackers to clean up the running back.

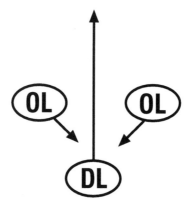

CHAPTER 4

PASS-RUSH DRILLS

DRILL #57: RABBIT

Objective: To develop the ability of defensive linemen to improve their get-off and their first step on a pass rush; to enhance the speed of the pass rush for defensive linemen who play on the edge.

Equipment Needed: A ball; a lined field.

Description: The coach positions a defensive lineman (#1, who is the rabbit) two yards off a yard line. He also positions another defensive lineman (#2) on the same yard line so that he is facing the first defensive lineman. On ball movement, defensive lineman #1 should backpedal as fast as he can. Defensive lineman #2 should try to touch #1 before the two of them reach the next five-yard line marker. The pair should repeat this maneuver five times and then switch roles, with #2 becoming the rabbit.

Coaching Points:

• The defensive linemen should move on ball movement.

• If defensive lineman #2 can capture the rabbit in this drill before reaching the five-yard marker, he will discover in a game situation that the offensive tackle will not be able to block his speed rush.

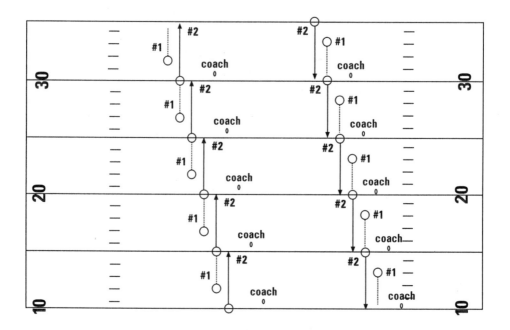

DRILL #58: TAKEOFFS

Objective: To develop the ability of defensive linemen to get off on ball movement while using a strong base and to maintain the discipline necessary to stay onside.

Equipment Needed: A football; a lined field.

Description: One to four defensive linemen crowd a football four yards from a yard line. The coach simulates an offensive center and barks out signals. Once the coach moves the ball, the defensive lineman should take an elongated step, emphasizing vertical push and bursting past the line.

Coaching Points:

- The defensive lineman should crowd the ball as much as possible without being offside.

- The coach should look for a toe to instep stagger about shoulder-width apart.

- The defensive lineman should have his inside hand down and inside foot back.

- The coach should watch the first step to make sure the defensive lineman actually takes a good, elongated first step, gaining ground vertically.

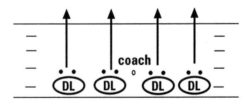

DRILL #59: GET-OFF

Objective: To develop the ability of pass-rushing defensive linemen to take a quick first step and to move on ball movement.

Equipment Needed: A tennis ball.

Description: The defensive lineman takes his elongated pass-rush stance on a yard line. The coach stands five yards away, holding the tennis ball as high as he can to one side of his body. When the coach drops the ball, the defensive lineman should attempt to catch the ball before it bounces on the ground a second time. As the player improves his quickness during this drill, the coach should move farther away than five yards.

Coaching Points:

- The player should burst as the ball leaves the coach's hand.

- The player should run low and stay over his knees.

- The player should strain and reach for his target.

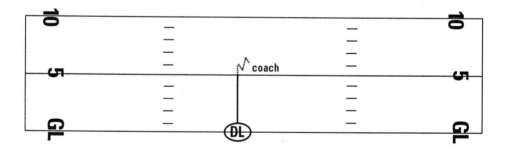

DRILL #60: SHORT WAVE "BREAK"

Objective: To teach and improve body control from a basic hitting position while rushing the quarterback and retracing to the screen.

Equipment Needed: Five agility bags; a football.

Description: The coach aligns four defensive linemen in a hole outside each bag. On the coach's command, each lineman should step up in the hole while keeping his feet moving. With each directional wave by the coach, they should step over the bag. When the coach simulates a quarterback throwing the football, the defensive linemen should rush him. The coach then throws the ball to a manager, and each lineman turns and bursts to the manager.

Coaching Points:

- The players should keep their weight over their knees and should assume the proper football position throughout this drill.

- The linemen should lead with their outside foot over each bag and should never cross over with their feet.

- The linemen should burst out of the bags toward the coach and keep their arms up as the ball is being released.

- The players should turn and again burst to the screen.

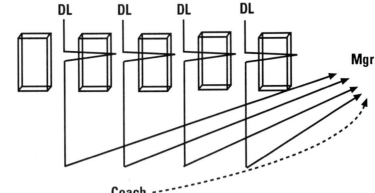

DRILL #61: ULTIMATE EFFORT

Objective: To develop the ability of defensive linemen to chase the football after it has been thrown.

Equipment Needed: A lined field; a football.

Description: The coach aligns the players in the defensive front in their positions and has them rush the passer on the snap of the ball. The coach simulates the actions of the quarterback by taking a five-step drop and throwing the ball to one of four stationary receivers. The defensive linemen should run to the spot of the throw until the other defenders get there. They should then break down and sprint off the field.

Coaching Points:

- The defensive linemen should keep their hands up to block the view of the coach.
- The linemen should turn and chase the football, all the while visualizing stripping the receiver from behind.

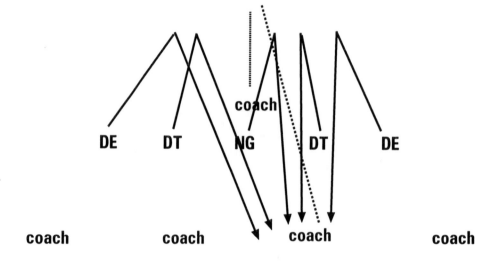

DRILL #62: INDICATOR

Objective: To develop the ability of defensive linemen to spot the quarterback's indicators and to determine what the quarterback's intentions are when he throws the football.

Equipment Needed: Two footballs.

Description: The coach positions the defensive linemen (in this case, the pass rushers), in their positions along the front. On ball movement, all the linemen should rush the quarterback at three-quarter speed. When the quarterback's indicators (i.e., his hands, his front arm, and the ball) reveal that he is going to throw the ball, the linemen should get their hands up and try to knock the ball down.

Coaching Points:

- As the quarterback's front hand comes off the football and his throwing motion begins, the linemen should start to raise their hands.

- If the ball is already out of the quarterback's hands, the defensive linemen may jump in an attempt to knock the ball down.

- To test the defensive linemen's discipline, the quarterback should use pump fakes.

- The linemen should not keep their arms up as they rush the quarterback.

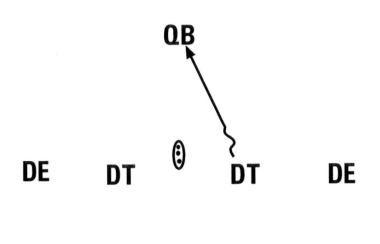

DRILL #63: HIGH STRIP

Objective: To develop the ability of pass rushers to stay on their feet as the quarterback starts his throwing motion.

Equipment Needed: Two footballs.

Description: The coach should align a defensive lineman in his normal position along the front. On ball movement, the lineman should rush the quarterback at three-quarter speed. As the quarterback throws the ball, the lineman should attempt a high strip.

Coaching Points:

- The defensive lineman should focus on the football in the quarterback's hands.
- When the quarterback puts the ball in his cocked throwing position, the defensive lineman should grab cloth with his front hand and attempt a high strip with his back hand.
- Whenever the lineman collapses on the quarterback, he should try to get to the quarterback's upfield shoulder.

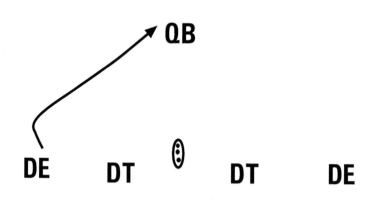

DRILL #64: OVER BAGS/RUSH REACTION

Objective: To help defensive linemen develop quick feet; to help them maintain proper body control; to help them improve their pass-rush reaction time.

Equipment Needed: Five agility bags; a hand shield.

Description: The hand shield, which the coach is holding, is the defensive lineman's target. On the coach's command, the lineman begins the drill by running through the bags one at a time, making sure to hit one foot in each hole. Once the lineman clears the last bag, the coach, who is facing him, moves the hand shield to either the right or the left. Depending on which direction the coach moves the hand shield, the lineman should step in that direction and perform a pass-rush move.

Coaching Points:

- The lineman should keep his weight over his knees as he runs through the bags.
- The lineman should concentrate on the hand shield, utilize the proper pass-rush technique, and then burst to the hand shield.

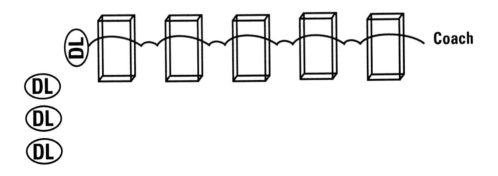

DRILL #65: HOOPS

Objective: To develop the ability of defensive linemen to get on the edge of a pass protector and run fishhooks around him in an effort to shorten the corner around him.

Equipment Needed: A painted circle or a circle of PVC pipe or a circle made out of a hose. (Although only one circle is needed for this drill, two circles will be needed for Drills #66 and #67. Therefore, the coach can save time by painting two circles on the field prior to this drill and then using both circles for the following two drills.)

Description: The coach positions a defensive lineman at a distance one yard outside the circle. On the coach's command, the lineman bursts around the circle twice—staying as close to the circle as he can.

Coaching Points:

- In order to stay as close to the circle as possible, the defensive lineman should try to lean into the circle as far as he can without falling.

- If the defensive lineman falls down, he should crab back up and continue running.

- When incorporating this lean on an offensive lineman, more times than not, he will keep the defensive lineman off the ground; in effect, he will be holding the defensive lineman up.

- This lean will give the offensive lineman no surface to punch, or block, the defensive lineman with, because the lean turns the shoulders sideways, making the pass rusher thin.

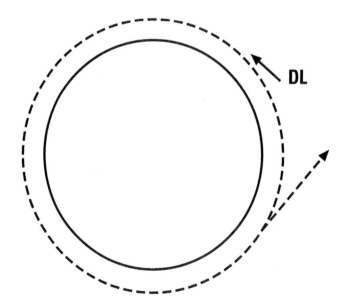

DRILL #66: FIGURE EIGHT

Objective: To develop the ability of a defensive lineman to attack an offensive lineman with enough speed to be able to get on an edge and run fishhooks.

Equipment Needed: Two painted circles or two circles of PVC pipe or two circles of hose.

Description: The coach positions a defensive lineman between the two circles and has him run a figure eight around the circles.

Coaching Points:

- The defensive lineman should burst out of his stance with an elongated first step.

- In order to stay as close to the two circles as possible, the defensive lineman should try to lean into the circle as far as he can without falling.

- As he approaches the second circle, the defensive lineman should transfer his weight and begin to lean the opposite way.

- When he has finished rounding the second circle, the defensive lineman should simulate a burst to the quarterback.

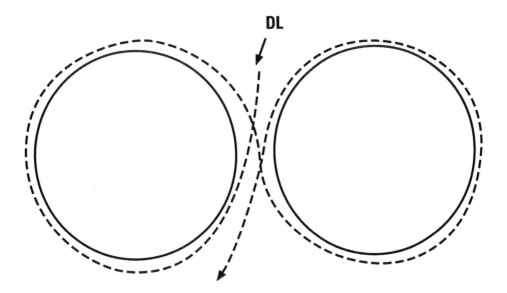

DRILL #67: CHASE

Objective: To enhance a defensive lineman's speed when attacking an offensive lineman in order to get on an edge and run fishhooks.

Equipment Needed: Two painted circles or two circles of PVC pipe or two circles of hose; a cone.

Description: The coach aligns two defensive linemen (#1 and #2) four yards apart, both facing the same direction. On the coach's command, the chaser (#2) tries to touch the rabbit (#1) before the rabbit performs a figure eight and touches the cone.

Coaching Points:

- The defenders should burst out of their stance with an elongated first step.

- When performing the figure eight, the chaser should lean as far into the circle as he can without falling so that he can stay close to the circles.

- If the chaser keeps it tight, he will make up enough ground to touch the rabbit.

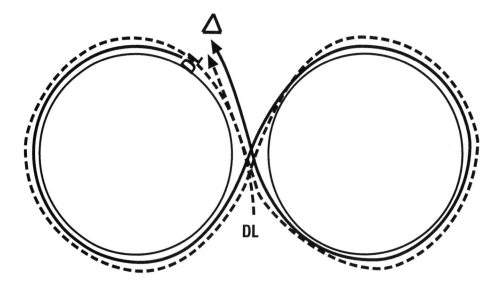

DRILL #68: PASS-RUSH TRANSITION

Objective: To teach get-off and the transition of pass-rush techniques going from one pass blocker to another; to teach counter-move techniques once the pass rusher gets beyond the depth of the quarterback.

Equipment Needed: Three bell dummies; a football.

Description: In this drill, the defensive linemen work one at a time. Each lineman gets off on ball movement and uses a different pass-rush move against each of the first two bell dummies. Once the defensive lineman reaches the third bell dummy, he should use a counter pass-rush technique and work back down to capture the quarterback. The coach should set up the bell dummies four yards apart and align the quarterback two yards in front of the last bell dummy.

Coaching Points:

- The defensive linemen should move on ball movement.

- The defensive linemen should use upper-body movement (i.e., shake and bake) on bell dummy No. 1 to simulate the action of setting up the first blocker.

- The defensive linemen should employ the pass-rush technique on bell dummy No. 1 and compress, or squeeze, the corner to the next blocker (i.e., bell dummy No. 2).

- The defensive linemen should use upper-body movement (shake and bake) to simulate the action of setting up the second blocker (bell dummy No. 2). They should also employ a pass-rush technique and compress the corner.

- Once the defensive lineman encounters the last bell dummy, he will find himself beyond the quarterback, which will require him to execute a counter pass-rush technique.

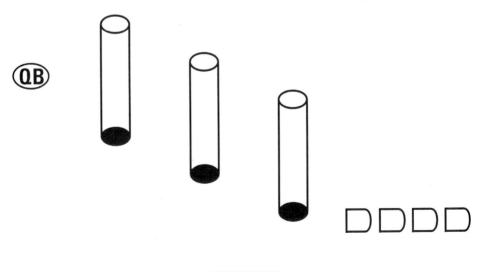

DRILL #69: GET-OFFS AGILITY BAG

Objective: To develop the ability of defensive linemen to get off on ball movement with a planned pass-rush move.

Equipment Needed: A football; five bell dummies.

Description: The coach aligns the players in their pass-rush positions. On the snap of the football, the players should perform a quick pass-rush move and then break either right or left, depending on the coach's direction.

Coaching Points:

- The defenders should key the ball movement.
- The defenders should have a plan in mind prior to the snap.
- The defenders should make their get-off and pass-rush moves quick and explosive.
- The defenders should burst down the line of scrimmage.

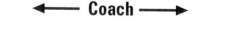

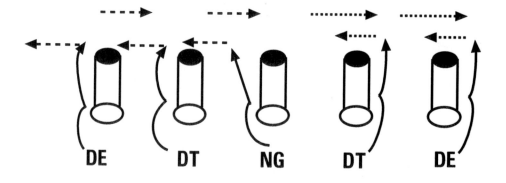

DRILL #70: SHAKE AND BAKE

Objective: To develop the ability of defensive linemen to use the proper upper-body movement before incorporating a pass-rush technique on a pass blocker.

Equipment Needed: Three bell dummies.

Description: The coach sets up his defensive linemen in one line. He then sends them—one at a time—through the bags, having them shake their shoulders and hands and patter their feet at each dummy before they incorporate a pass-rush move.

Coaching Points:

- The defenders should take the time to overexaggerate their hand and shoulder movements before each dummy.

- The defenders should practice different pass-rush techniques on each individual dummy.

- The coach should find it beneficial to have his players incorporate a spin move on the last dummy, because the spin move is the hardest move for the defensive lineman to master.

DL

DRILL #71: NINJA

Objective: To develop the ability of defensive linemen to use the proper technique of spinning when rushing the passer.

Equipment Needed: Three bell dummies.

Description: The coach sets up the defensive linemen in a single-file line facing the bell dummies. On the coach's command, one player at a time should approach each dummy and perform three consecutive spin moves on each one.

Coaching Points:

- The players should sink their hips as they approach each dummy.

- The players should plant their outside foot and drive off of it.

- The players should cup the hand of their outside arm and violently swing the arm around and catch the bag. We call this maneuver a ninja.

- The players should keep their feet moving and approach each bag performing their spin in the opposite direction.

- When using a spin move, the off, or outside, hand (ninja) of the defender is the key to separation and also to propelling the rusher toward the quarterback.

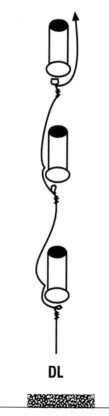

DL

DRILL #72: OVER-RUSH COUNTER

Objective: To develop the ability of rush men to use the proper technique of counter moving when they are pushed past the quarterback by an offensive lineman.

Equipment Needed: A bell dummy.

Description: The coach positions a defensive lineman so that he is shaded on an offensive lineman. In this drill, the defensive lineman should speed-rush up the field and engage the offensive lineman. Once he feels himself being pushed past the bell dummy (i.e., the simulated quarterback), the defender should stop and spin back under.

Coaching Points:

- The defensive lineman should make sure he has some width in his shaded position off of the offensive lineman in his initial alignment.

- The defender should make sure his first step is explosive and elongated.

- Once he makes contact with the offensive lineman, the defender should get his eyes inside and find the quarterback.

- As he spins under, the defender should stop and drop his hips.

- The defender should use his off hand as a whip to create separation from the offensive lineman and propel himself toward the quarterback.

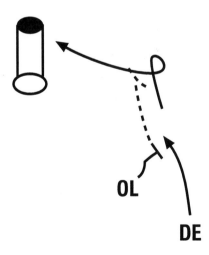

DRILL #73: WIDE-RUSH COUNTER

Objective: To develop the ability of defensive linemen to successfully counter spin when they are knocked out of their pass-rush lane.

Equipment Needed: A bell dummy.

Description: The coach aligns a defensive lineman so that he is shaded on an offensive lineman. The offensive lineman begins the drill by jump setting (attacking) the defensive lineman and starting to push him wide. When the defensive lineman feels he is too wide, he should counter spin back under.

Coaching Points:

- The defender should learn to have a feel for being out of the proper pass-rush lane.

- Once the offensive lineman and the defensive lineman have gained some momentum moving sideways, the spin by the defensive lineman will use the offensive lineman's momentum against him.

- The defensive lineman should remember to drop his hips and stop before he spins.

- When he uses his off hand as a whip, the defender should make sure he opens his hips and his palm. Next, he should slap his palm against the offensive lineman's back in order to create separation and to propel himself into the quarterback.

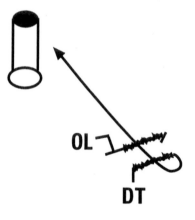

DRILL #74: PASS RUSH

Objective: To develop the ability of defenders to use the proper pass-rush technique and pass-rush lanes.

Equipment Needed: A lined pass-rush field; a football.

Description: In this drill, the coach has the defensive linemen work one at a time on reacting to the snap of the ball. In order to keep the defensive linemen honest, the coach should have the offense change up the snap count.

Coaching Points:

- The defensive linemen should have a plan in mind before the snap.

- The defensive linemen should get off on ball movement and attack the pass set with an effective, explosive first step.

- The defensive linemen should execute a pass-rush move, eliminating their hand and arm to the side of the protector that the defensive linemen are going to rush.

- Each defender should find a way to get on top of his blocker (or behind him).

- The defenders should try to execute as many counter moves as possible until they get to the quarterback—even if their initial move does not work.

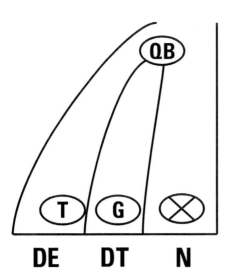
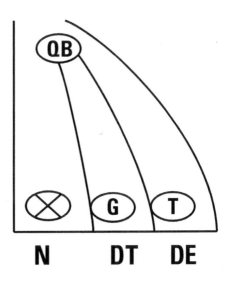

DRILL #75: STUNT

Objective: To develop the ability of a pass rusher to use the proper techniques while moving with another pass rusher into a new pass-rush lane; to help him use proper spacing in the newly created pass-rush lanes.

Equipment Needed: A pass-rush lined field; a football.

Description: The coach should work the stunts with two or three defensive linemen at a time. The coach should have the offense change up the snap count in order to keep the defensive linemen honest.

Coaching Points:

• The pass rushers should learn to get off on ball movement together.

• The pass rushers should come as tight as they can on the stunt, making sure not to waste any steps.

• The pass rushers should try to keep from getting pushed out of their pass-rush lane and make sure everything is working vertically in their stunt.

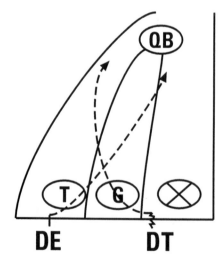 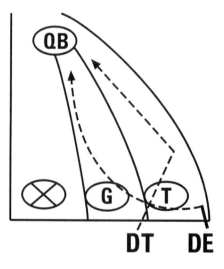

DRILL #76: PLAY-ACTION PASS RUSH

Objective: To develop the ability of defensive ends to pick up the angles of the backs and to use the proper series of actions that will enable them to become important factors in the pass rush.

Equipment Needed: A strip (hose); a football.

Description: As this drill plays out, the tight end should release into a pass route. The fullback should come on a 45-degree angle and block the defensive end with either a cut block or a high block. The quarterback should then set up to pass behind the fullback.

Coaching Points:

- When the defensive end is aligned over the tight end, he should key the tight end's helmet and then take a mirror step with the tight end's release into the pass route.

- Once the tight end is no longer a threat to block the defensive end, he should find the next key (the fullback) and execute the proper pass-rush technique and capture the quarterback.

- The defensive end should key the fullback's helmet for either a high block or a cut block.

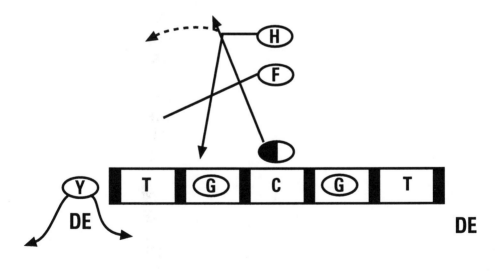

DRILL #77: PEEL

Objective: To develop the ability of defensive ends to use the proper contain rush technique against the sprint-out and to successfully play blockers at their feet.

Equipment Needed: A ball; a hose or a strip.

Description: In this drill, the tight end should release into a route, while the offensive tackle reach blocks the defensive end. The fullback should try to either cut block or roll block the defensive end. The tailback should try to hook the defensive end. Meanwhile, the quarterback has the ball and should try to beat the defender outside, breaking contain.

Coaching Points:

- The coach should consider this drill a low-tempo technique drill for defensive ends.

- The defensive end should keep his eyes on the blocker until he defeats the blocker.

- The defensive end should get upfield as quickly as possible and attack the second back, who is the tailback.

- The defender should keep his blocker on his inside half.

- The defensive end should keep the blockers on his inside half.

- The defensive end should keep his pads parallel to the line of scrimmage with his weight down.

- The defensive end should use his hands on the cut and roll blocks, peeling off of the series of blocks he encounters and keeping the quarterback in the pocket.

- As the defensive end peels off of the tailback, he should work to make the tackle on the quarterback.

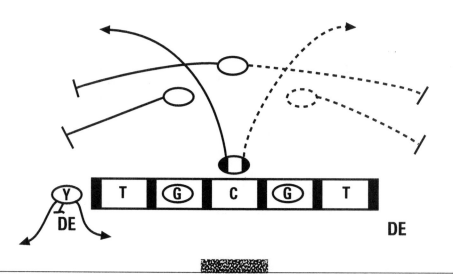

DRILL #78: SPRINT-OUT

Objective: To develop the ability of defensive ends to defeat the cut block.

Equipment Needed: A strip or a hose.

Description: Although the coach can run this drill using only defensive players, he will find it more beneficial to use offensive players as well. In this drill, the defensive end has to play off of two cut blocks and keep the quarterback from sprinting out. Even though the coach has the option of using an offensive lineman, he may be better off using that block as a low-tempo type of block. The next series of cut blockers—the two running backs—should go at full speed.

Coaching Points:

- The coach should never do this drill live without first doing some sort of cut-block drill at low tempo.

- The defensive end should keep his chest over his knees, his tail down, and his feet moving.

- The defensive end should attack the upfield back and make the first back come find him.

- The coach should make sure the defensive end sees high hat/low hat.

- If the defensive end gets a low hat (or a low cut), he should use his hands to slow down the blocker's charge and keep the blocker clear of his outside leg. If the defensive end keeps his shoulders square to the line of scrimmage, he will also help keep the running back from his outside leg.

- In order to gain ground on the quarterback, the defensive end should give ground on the running back.

- If he sees a high hat or a kick-out block, the defensive end should perform either a shoulder forearm lift or a rip technique.

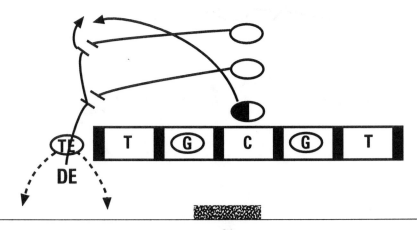

DRILL #79: PASS RUSH: DEFENSIVE ENDS VS. BACKS

Objective: To teach defensive ends proper pass-rush techniques versus running backs.

Equipment Needed: A strip or a hose; a bell dummy; a football.

Description: The coach should align the defensive end on the edge of the hose. He should also position a running back four yards deep in the backfield and a bell dummy seven yards deep in the backfield. On the snap of the football, the running back should pass protect the bell dummy for three seconds. (A timer is needed, allowing the defensive end to capture the bell dummy.)

Coaching Points:

- The defensive end's initial aiming point on his pass rush should be the inside half of the running back's body.

- The defensive end should employ a pass-rush move on the outside half of the running back's body, keeping his contain pass-rush lane.

- The defensive end should begin to employ his pass-rush move sooner than normal on a running back, because running backs have a tendency to lunge at defensive ends.

- If the defensive end finds the running back stationary and not lunging, he should use a power bull-rush move to the bell dummy.

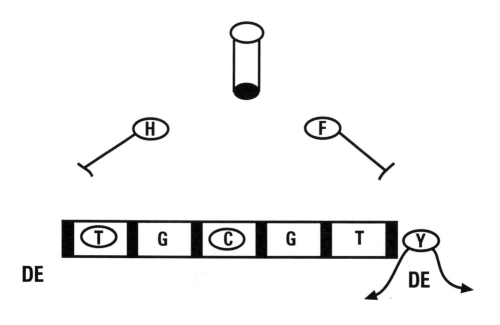

DRILL #80: PASS RUSH: DEFENSIVE ENDS VS. TIGHT ENDS

Objective: To develop the ability of defensive ends to find different pathways and angles to the quarterback when they are covered up by the tight end.

Equipment Needed: A strip or a hose; a bell dummy.

Description: The coach sets up the drill by positioning a tight end on the end of the strip in a tight end alignment. The coach then puts the defensive end head-up on the tight end. On the coach's command, the tight end should move. The defensive end should then either rush the passer or play run versus an aggressive tight end block.

Coaching Points:

- The defensive end should key the tight end's helmet for movement.

- If the tight end aggressively blocks the defensive end, the defensive end should get his vision back inside for either a run or a pass key.

- If the defensive end sees a pass key, he should perform a power move with a pull to clear himself from the tight end. If the tight end pass sets, the defensive end should work on the outside half of the tight end's body with pass-rush moves.

- If the tight end sets up really deep (two yards or more), the defensive end should undercut him inside with a pass-rush move and then work back up the field for contain.

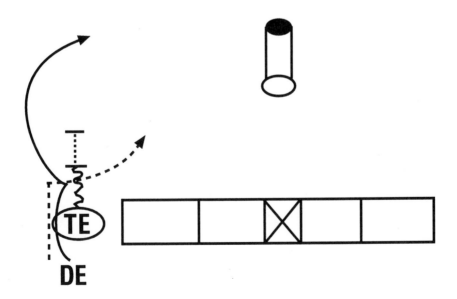

DRILL #81: DEFENSIVE END MAN-TO-MAN

Objective: To develop the ability of defensive ends to successfully play the tight end man-to-man on blitzes.

Equipment Needed: A football.

Description: The coach aligns the defensive end over a tight end. The coach stands behind the defensive end and either tells the tight end what route to run or instructs him to block the defensive end. The defensive end should play both run and pass while covering the tight end man-to-man.

Coaching Points:

- The defensive end should attack the tight end by first using the proper technique for the run.

- Some tight ends give away run/pass by their pre-snap alignments. The tight end should split out away from his offensive tackle in order to get a more effective release into his pass route (i.e., split out to get out).

- The defensive end should prevent the tight end's inside release so he has only one way to go—outside.

- The defensive end should get in the tight end's hip pocket and run with him. The defensive end should never look back for the football, because by doing so, he will create separation.

- If the tight end's hands go up, the defensive end should clap the tight end's outside hand with his own outside hand and grab cloth with his other hand, ensuring the tackle.

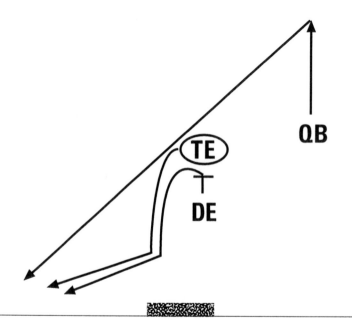

DRILL #82: ANTI-DRAW

Objective: To develop the ability of defensive linemen to retrace their steps on the draw play (to hasten their reaction time to a pass set versus a draw read, commonly known as a "throw-by").

Equipment Needed: A football.

Description: The coach lines up his defensive linemen over four offensive linemen and stands behind the defensive linemen. The coach instructs the offense to either pass set or quick set, thus inviting the defensive linemen to take a direct path to the quarterback for a draw play. The defensive linemen should react to what they see.

Coaching Points:

- The defensive linemen should get off on ball movement with an elongated first step.

- Each defensive lineman should key the inside (or post) foot of the offensive lineman over him. If the foot stays stationary and the offensive lineman's hips are open, the defensive lineman should read draw.

- If the offensive lineman kicks back as he tries to cover up the defensive lineman, the defender should rush the passer.

- If a draw read is given, the defensive linemen should either retrace their steps or come back down their stem. (In other words, the defensive linemen should go out the way they came in.)

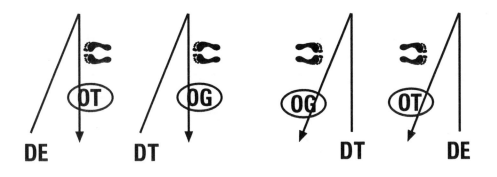

DRILL #83: THREE-STEP CUT

Objective: To develop the ability of defensive ends to keep their hands up while getting cut by a running back on three-step drops by the quarterback.

Equipment Needed: A football.

Description: The coach aligns a defensive end over an offensive tackle and has the tackle either block down or cut the end. The coach has the running back go and cut the defensive end on all down blocks by the offensive tackle. The coach tells the offense what blocking scheme to incorporate and instructs the defensive end to stay on his feet and try to knock the ball down.

Coaching Points:

- The defensive end should position himself in the throwing lane with his first two steps.

- The defensive end should show quick reaction time to the running back if the offensive tackle blocks down.

- The defensive end should get vertical and move into the throwing lane as he is being cut by the running back.

- If the cut block occurs and the defensive end is successful in taking away the throw and the quarterback pulls the ball down, the defensive end should be active and keep himself off of the ground.

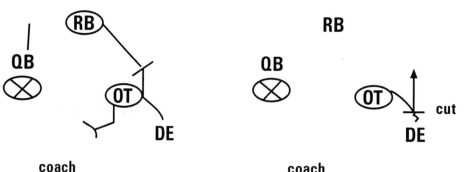

DRILL #84: PENETRATION RUSH

Objective: To develop the ability of defensive linemen to properly blow a gap in third-and-long situations.

Equipment Needed: Two hand shields; a football.

Description: The coach aligns a defensive lineman in an elongated three-point pass-rush stance between two players with hand shields on their inside arms. On the snap of the ball, the defensive lineman should split the two shields and get vertical up the field as fast as possible.

Coaching Points:

- The defensive lineman should key the football for movement.

- The defensive lineman's first elongated step should take him to the other side of the line of scrimmage.

- The defensive lineman should turn his upper torso so that he provides only a small blocking surface.

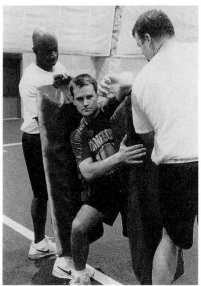

DRILL #85: POWER-RUSH SIT

Objective: To teach defensive linemen to feel when an offensive lineman braces, or sits, in his pass protection, and to use the offensive lineman's body against him.

Equipment Needed: None.

Description: The coach fits up both an offensive and a defensive lineman in a two-point bull-rush position. The coach has the defensive lineman close his eyes and start walking the offensive lineman backwards. After a few steps, the offensive lineman braces himself (i.e., sits) against the defensive lineman. When the defender feels his momentum stop, he should yank the offensive lineman's jersey and throw himself by him.

Coaching Points:

- The defensive lineman should be lower than the offensive lineman, with his face buried in the offensive lineman's chest.

- The "throw-by" must be simultaneous with the "sit" so that the defensive lineman can use the offensive lineman's weight against him.

- In order to get off of the block cleanly, the defensive lineman must make his "throw" quick and violent.

DRILL #86: FINAL-PHASE ACCELERATION

Objective: To rehearse the last phase of maneuver in which the defensive lineman gets on top of the offensive lineman and accelerates to the quarterback.

Equipment Needed: A bell dummy.

Description: The coach positions the defensive lineman in a two-point stance, parallel to the offensive lineman and straddling his body at the start of the drill. On the coach's command, the defensive lineman should finish his pass-rush move and get on top of the offensive lineman and accelerate to the quarterback.

Coaching Points:

• The defensive lineman should perform a pass-rush technique that will get him one yard behind the offensive lineman.

• The defensive lineman should get on top of the offensive lineman so he has no chance to recover.

• The defensive lineman should get his shoulders square to the quarterback as soon as he has cleared the offensive lineman.

• The defensive end should accelerate low and keep his weight forward.

DRILL #87: RECOVER AND RUSH

Objective: To develop the ability of defensive linemen to get up off the ground after being cut, encounter a second blocker, and capture the quarterback.

Equipment Needed: A bell dummy.

Description: The coach has a defensive lineman lie on his back, with his head facing the line of scrimmage. On the coach's command, the player should get up off the ground, defeat the running back, and capture the quarterback.

Coaching Points:

- The defensive lineman should pop up off the ground quickly.

- The defensive lineman should use a power-rush technique when rushing a running back.

- Also when rushing a running back, the defensive lineman should use a finesse move as his change-up.

DRILL #88: BODY-TO-BODY RUSH

Objective: To develop the ability of defensive linemen to use proper leverage and power angles when going body-to-body on a power-rush move.

Equipment Needed: A bell dummy.

Description: The coach fits up both an offensive and a defensive lineman in a two-point bull-rush position. The coach positions the two players five yards from the bell dummy and points the defensive lineman in the direction of the dummy. On the coach's command, the defensive lineman should try to drive the offensive lineman into the bell dummy.

Coaching Points:

- The defensive lineman should fit up on the offensive lineman with his face mask in the offensive lineman's chest.

- The defensive lineman should have the proper bend in his knees and should keep his hands inside on the offensive lineman's chest plate.

- The defensive lineman should roll his hips for power, lock out his arms for separation, and drive his feet.

- If a stalemate occurs, the defensive lineman should yank the offensive lineman's jersey and throw himself by him.

- If momentum is in his favor, the defensive lineman should strain and continue to drive the offensive lineman into the bell dummy.

DRILL #89: KNOCK 'EM AWAY

Objective: To develop the ability of the defensive lineman to concentrate on the offensive lineman's punch on pass protection and eliminate the offensive lineman's hands.

Equipment Needed: None.

Description: The coach aligns a defensive lineman over an offensive lineman, with each of them in a two-point stance. The drill begins with the offensive lineman trying to punch the defensive lineman in the chest. The defensive lineman should react to this punch by knocking away the offensive lineman's hands and getting on top of or behind the offensive lineman.

Coaching Points:

- The defensive lineman should concentrate on the elbows of the offensive lineman, since most offensive linemen cock their elbows before they punch.

- The defensive lineman should use a two-hand knock-to-the-side technique.

- The defensive lineman should use a two-hand knockdown technique.

- The defensive lineman should use a two-hand knockout technique (splitting his hands).

- The defensive lineman should practice getting on top of the offensive lineman after every technique.

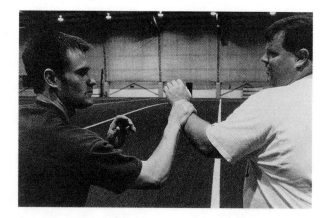

DRILL #90: NOSEGUARD GAUNTLET

Objective: To develop the ability of the noseguard to use the proper fundamentals in defeating a double-team on pass protection against the center and the offensive guard and in defeating a third blocker and capturing the quarterback.

Equipment Needed: A bell dummy; a football.

Description: The coach aligns the noseguard between two offensive linemen. On the snap of the ball, the noseguard should try to defeat the initial double-team and the running back. The running back, who is five yards deep, should start his block when the noseguard clears the first two blockers. The drill does not end until the noseguard has touched the bell dummy.

Coaching Points:

- The noseguard should have the mind-set that three people cannot control a determined player.

- The noseguard should attack and defeat the man who is double-teaming him first— the guard.

- In order to stay in his pass-rush lane, the noseguard should try to split the offensive linemen.

- By splitting the offensive linemen, the noseguard will put himself on the edge of the post blocker, who is the center.

- The coach should emphasize to the noseguard that this drill is an effort drill and that he should never quit. (The noseguard never knows how long the quarterback will hold the ball and, consequently, how long the noseguard will be a factor in the play.)

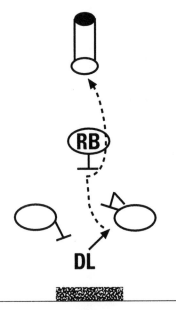

CHAPTER 5

MOVEMENT DRILLS

DRILL #91: CHANGE OF DIRECTION/FUMBLE RECOVERY

Objective: To improve the ability of the defensive lineman to change direction; to enhance his agility from a basic football position; to enhance his foot quickness, teaching him to bounce up off the ground after being knocked down and to recover a fumble properly.

Equipment Needed: Six agility bags; a football.

Description: The coach should give a "Feet" command, which tells the defensive lineman his feet should be live and chopping in one spot. On the coach's signal, the defensive lineman should move laterally with his outside foot, changing direction over the bags. Once the coach sends the defensive lineman over the last bag, the lineman should perform a seat roll and recover a fumble.

Coaching Points:

- The defensive lineman should start in the proper football position and stay there throughout the drill, keeping his eyes up.

- The defensive lineman should not cross over. He should change directions as quickly as he can while maintaining good arm action.

- When the defensive lineman executes his seat roll, he should bounce up off the ground, using his hands to help him get up.

- When the defensive lineman recovers the fumbled football, he should grab it with two hands, pulling it in and seating it into his midsection with his chin tucked and his top leg protecting the football. The defensive lineman should end up in a fetal position, with a firm lock on the football.

- The defensive lineman should not jump, roll, or dive on top of the football.

DRILL #92: FIT/ESCAPE FUMBLE RECOVERY

Objective: To develop the ability of defensive linemen to use the proper technique of recovering a fumble in tight quarters.

Equipment Needed: A football.

Description: The coach aligns a defensive lineman over an offensive lineman. The coach instructs the defensive lineman to fit up on the offensive lineman and then disengage and recover the fumble by the coach.

Coaching Points:

- When the defensive lineman sees the ball on the ground, he should violently throw, or get rid of, the offensive lineman so he can escape cleanly.

- The defensive lineman should reach for the football and pull it in, seating it in the midsection of his body, with his top arm and leg covering it.

- The defensive lineman should not jump on the football, roll it, or expose it in tight quarters.

DRILL #93: STRIP

Objective: To develop the ability of defenders to properly strip the football.

Equipment Needed: A football.

Description: The coach instructs a ball carrier to put the football in a locked position under his arm. The coach then instructs a defensive lineman to stand behind the ball carrier. On the coach's command of "Fit!" the defender takes his hand to the ball and cups the point of it. He takes his other hand and wraps it over the opposite shoulder of the ball carrier and grabs cloth to ensure the tackle. On the coach's "Strip" command, the defender pulls the football back toward him, stripping it out.

Coaching Points:

- The defender should make sure his hand is under the football all the way to the point of the football.

- The coach should emphasize to his defensive players that the most important aspect of this drill is that the defender ensure the tackle of the ball carrier by using both his off hand and his off arm.

- The defender should be violent when he strips the ball out.

DRILL #94: ESCAPE FROM SAIGON

Objective: To develop the ability of defensive linemen to steal the football when they are in a pile and out of the referee's view.

Equipment Needed: A football.

Description: In this drill, the coach challenges all of his defensive linemen to steal the football from him. One player is instructed to steal the football, while everyone else piles on.

Coaching Points:

- The defensive linemen should remember to be violent with their strip moves.

- This drill is a fun teaching tool for everyone, because it pits the players against the coach.

- The coach had better not be out of shape!

DRILL #95: DOWN THE LINE

Objective: To develop the ability of defensive linemen to use proper straight-line movements when stunting, as well as to maintain flexibility in their hips; to develop their ability to turn their knees during the redirection phase of stunting.

Equipment Needed: Five agility bags; a cone.

Description: The coach lays five bags on the ground, one yard apart, and places a cone two yards off the second bag. On the coach's command, the defensive linemen should step over the bags, hitting both feet down in every hole. Once they clear the last bag, the players should plant their outside foot, turn their knees and their hips toward the cone, and burst underneath the cone.

Coaching Points:

- The players should maintain a proper, low base while stepping over the bags and should make sure they lead with their onside foot and hit both feet down quickly between the bags.

- When clearing the last bag, the players should concentrate on turning both their knees toward the cone to eliminate wasted motion.

- The more proficient the players become at doing this drill, the tighter the cone can be moved toward the bag. This adjustment will force the players to make sharper cuts.

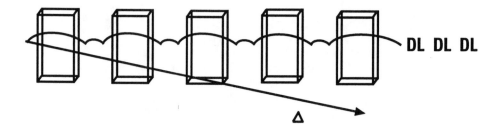

DRILL #96: TWIST

Objective: To develop the ability of defensive linemen to use the proper steps and the proper timing while moving, and to find the football as they cross the line of scrimmage.

Equipment Needed: Five bell dummies; a football.

Description: The coach sets up five bell dummies representing the offensive line and positions a ball carrier five yards deep. On the coach's command, the ball carrier should shuffle either right or left and then run between the bell dummies as the defensive line performs its movement or stunt. Once the defensive linemen clear the line of scrimmage, they must locate the football and run to it.

Coaching Points:

- Anytime the defensive linemen perform movement, they must stay low and be quick.

- If more than one defensive lineman is involved in a movement, the whole defensive line must practice its timing to make sure everyone is moving properly.

- The defensive linemen should never do a movement drill unless they are able to use a ball carrier in the drill.

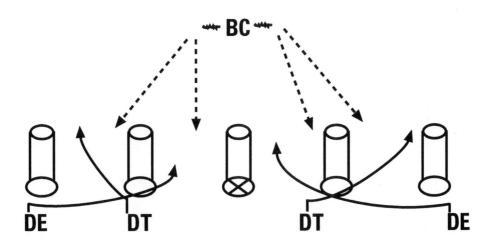

DRILL #97: STUNT GRAB/PICK

Objective: To improve the timing and location of two-man stunts when a twister (i.e., a twisting defensive lineman) is grabbing an offensive lineman to free up a looper (i.e., a looping defensive lineman).

Equipment Needed: A lined pass-rush field; a football.

Description: The coach positions two defensive linemen in their proper alignments head-up on two offensive linemen. On the snap of the ball, the defensive linemen should perform the stunt called for by the coach—one half of the stunt being performed by a twister and the other half being performed by a looper.

Coaching Points:

- The post twister's aiming point should be either the top or the bottom half of the person he is going to grab.

- When contact is made, the hands of the twister should be tight to his body.

- The looper has to be patient until the twister slices through into the backfield.

- After seeing the twister slice into the backfield, the looper should come as tight as possible to the twister, thus creating the pick situation.

DRILL #98: SLANT/ANGLE

Objective: To develop the ability of defensive linemen to slant (or angle) in unison on the snap of the ball.

Equipment Needed: A strip or a hose; five bell dummies; a football.

Description: The coach should have all of his players in the defensive front line perform this drill so they can sharpen their timing and understand their gap responsibilities. The coach sets up the drill by aligning these players in their shaded techniques. On the snap of the ball, the players should slant and get vertical off of the bell dummies.

Coaching Points:

- On the snap of the football, each defensive lineman should take a lateral step toward the line of scrimmage.

- The second step taken by the lineman should be vertical through the inside half of the offensive lineman so he maintains gap control.

- The coach can change up this drill by having the defensive linemen slant in either direction.

- The coach can also add linebackers and running backs to this drill so that all the defensive players can get a clear, true picture of everybody's gap control.

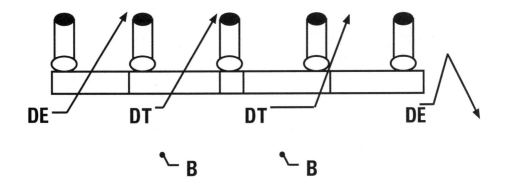

DRILL #99: PINCH

Objective: To develop the ability of defensive linemen to use the proper steps and the proper techniques when pinching gaps in short-yardage and goal-line situations.

Equipment Needed: A strip or a hose; five bell dummies; a football.

Description: The coach should have all of his players in the defensive front line perform this drill so they can better understand their responsibilities. In setting up the drill, the coach positions the defensive linemen in their shaded techniques. On the coach's command, the linemen should pinch their inside gap and get vertical. By adding linebackers and running backs to the drill, the coach will help his players get a clear, true picture of all the gaps being canceled.

Coaching Points:

- The first step taken by the defensive linemen should be lateral and toward the line of scrimmage.

- The second step taken by the defensive linemen should be vertical through the inside half of the offensive linemen so they can maintain inside gap control.

- The defenders should discover that by making either an uppercut or a rip move, they will have better power angles when encountering a blocker.

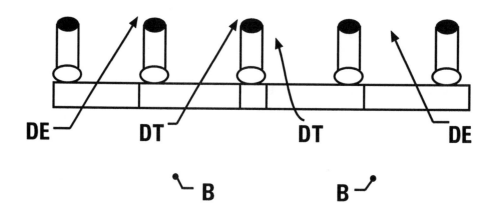

DRILL #100: DEFENSIVE TACKLE ZONE DOG

Objective: To develop the ability of defensive tackles to drop and find the crossing receivers when called upon to drop in a zone blitz.

Equipment Needed: A football.

Description: The coach aligns a defensive tackle in his proper technique in the defense called for. The coach then instructs the offensive lineman to either run block or pass set. The receivers run intermediate and under routes (i.e., shallow crossing routes) from different sides. The defensive tackle should either find the under route and eliminate it, or get into the throwing lane of the quarterback.

Coaching Points:

- The defensive tackle should clear run first and make sure he does not get knocked off of the line of scrimmage.

- The defensive tackle should open his hips in the proper direction required and burst as deep as possible before the quarterback sets up.

- The defensive tackle should get his head on a swivel and look both ways for shallow crossers.

- The defensive tackle should get a good break on the football as soon as the quarterback throws it.

- If the defensive tackle does not encounter a shallow crosser, he should spy, or mirror, the quarterback so he can defend against the scramble.

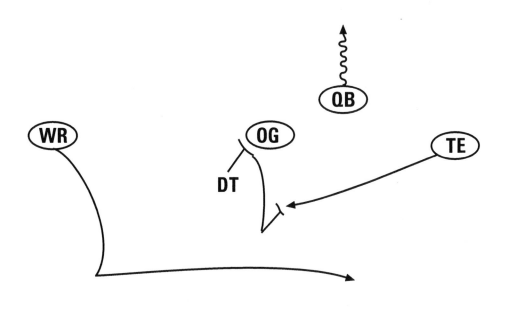

DRILL #101: DEFENSIVE END ZONE DOG

Objective: To develop the ability of defensive ends to angle, clear run, and burst to the out/flat/flare area.

Equipment Needed: A lined field; a football.

Description: The coach aligns the defensive end in his proper position. On the snap of the ball, the defensive end should angle and burst to the out/flat/flare area and play the routes he sees. As he oversees the drill, the coach should stand behind the defensive end and instruct the wide receiver and the running back on what route combinations he wants them to run.

Coaching Points:

- The defensive end should clear all the blockers and play run first.

- The defensive end should turn his hips on a 45-degree angle and burst 10–12 yards deep, just outside the numbers on the football field.

- The defensive end should be able to see the quarterback and be ready to break on the quarterback's intentions or throwing motion to any receiver in his zone.

- The defensive end should play the deepest receiver first and then break on anything thrown underneath.

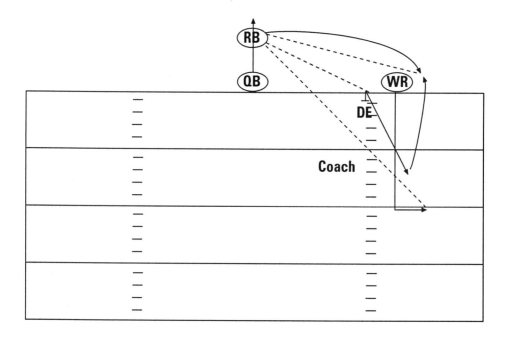

Mark Snyder is the defensive ends coach at the University of Minnesota. Since assuming his present position in 1997, Snyder has put his mark on the Gophers' football program. Under his guidance, defensive end Lamanzer Williams tied for first in the country with 18.5 sacks last fall en route to collecting first-team All-America honors. It marked the first time since 1971 that a Golden Gopher had received that honor.

Behind the coaching of Snyder and the stellar play of Williams, Minnesota stood atop the Big Ten with a single-season school record of 41 sacks in 1997 and finished fifth overall in the Big Ten in total defense. It was the highest league ranking by the Gophers since 1985.

A member of Division I-AA Youngstown State's staff from 1991 to 1996, Snyder was named defensive coordinator in 1996. During the 1995 season, Snyder was the school's inside linebackers/special teams coordinator. In addition to serving as Youngstown's outside linebackers coach in 1993–94, he headed the Penguins' punt-block unit that was responsible for blocking an amazing 14 punts in two seasons.

During Snyder's six years at Youngstown State, the Penguins advanced to the NCAA Division I-AA championship game four consecutive years and captured three national crowns.

Snyder's coaching career began in 1988 at his alma mater, Marshall University. He spent the next two seasons at Central Florida.

A 1987 graduate of Marshall, Snyder capped an impressive collegiate career when, as a senior, he helped lead the Thundering Herd to the I-AA national title game, where they dropped a heartbreaking 43-42 decision to Northeast Louisiana. He earned All-America honors as a defensive back that season and, at the time, was the Southern Conference's all-time interception leader with 10 picks.

Prior to his enrollment at Marshall, Snyder attended Northeast Oklahoma A&M Junior College, where he helped lead the Golden Norsemen to the NJCAA national title game as a quarterback. He is a native of Ironton, Ohio.

Snyder and his wife, Beth, have two daughters, Chelsea Elizabeth and Lindsay Nicole. They reside in Woodbury, Minnesota.

ADDITIONAL FOOTBALL RESOURCES FROM